MYRTLEFIELD
HOUSE

Key Bible Concepts

Myrtlefield Encounters

Myrtlefield Encounters are complementary studies of biblical literature, Christian teaching and apologetics. The books in this series engage the minds of believers and sceptics. They show how God has spoken in the Bible to address the realities of life and its questions, problems, beauty and potential.

Books in this series:

Key Bible Concepts: Defining the Basic Terms of the Christian Faith

Christianity: Opium or Truth?: Answering Thoughtful Objections to the Christian Faith

The Definition of Christianity: Exploring the Original Meaning of the Christian Faith

The Bible and Ethics: Finding the Moral Foundations of the Christian Faith

Key Bible Concepts

Defining the Basic Terms
of the Christian Faith

David Gooding

John Lennox

Myrtlefield Encounters

Cover design: Matthew Craig.

Originally published as a series of articles in the Russian newspaper, *Uchitelskaya Gazeta*.

First published in English in 1997.

Published by The Myrtlefield Trust
PO BOX 2216, Belfast, BT1 9YR
w: www.myrtlefieldhouse.com
e: info@myrtlefieldhouse.com

ISBN: 978-1-874584-45-2 (pbk.)
ISBN: 978-1-874584-46-9 (PDF)
ISBN: 978-1-874584-47-6 (Kindle)
ISBN: 978-1-874584-48-3 (EPUB without DRM)

24 23 22 21 20 19   12 11 10 9 8

Contents

1. Introduction   1
2. Holiness: God's Majesty, Purity, Beauty, and Love   11
3. Sin: A Disease, Its Symptoms and Its Cure   20
4. Reconciliation: The Way to Peace   29
5. Justification: Getting Things Legally Right   38
6. Ransom and Redemption: The Price of Freedom   47
7. Eternal Life: In the Here and Now   56
8. Repentance: More than Being Sorry   65
9. Faith: Not a Leap in the Dark   74
10. Faith: A Response to Evidence   83
11. Faith: A Question of Whom You Trust   101
12. Sanctification: Like Father, Like Son   110
13. Sanctification: Sonship Not Slavery   119
14. The Final Judgment: The Demands of Justice   128
15. The Final Judgment: The Goodness and
    Severity of God   138
16. Salvation: The Great Comprehensive Term   148
    Scripture Index   159
    Other books by David Gooding and John Lennox   165
    The Quest for Reality and Significance   166
    About the Authors   184

CHAPTER 1

Introduction

No one can call himself truly educated without some acquaintance with the Bible, which has had, and still has, such a profound impact on world thought. It was the first major book ever printed and the first in movable type (in a Latin translation on Gutenberg's press in Mainz, Germany, in 1455). No other book has been read by more people and published in more languages than the Bible.

As we read it, we shall come across words and concepts which, though in some sense familiar, we do not immediately understand since they are being used as technical terms. This should not blunt our interest—rather the reverse, it should increase it. For in this modern world we all sooner or later have to learn the meaning of technical terms in one or more fields of knowledge, and it is in the understanding of those terms that the real interest lies. Someone who wants to be a good cook must learn the difference between roasting, grilling, frying, poaching and boiling, and why you would use one process with some foods and another with others. Someone who aims to be a motor mechanic must know what a piston is, and a carburettor, and a cylinder; the difference between a petrol engine and a diesel engine; and what clutches, gears, and accelerators are for. And all of us who learn to use computers find ourselves confronted by a whole array of terms which we need to master.

As in any other field, it is in getting to grips with the technical terms in the Bible that leads not only to deeper understanding of them but also to an increased ability to communicate their meaning to others, thus opening a window for them on a whole new world.

So in these few chapters we shall be studying these technical terms, and in this introduction we shall briefly survey the ground we intend to cover.

Holiness

The logical place to start is with God and since one of the most important terms which describes God is 'holy' we shall start with that. However, just here we might meet an objection. 'I don't believe in God,' says someone; 'so I am not interested in his holiness, whatever that may mean. I live my life without acknowledging any god whatever.'

Well, those are very interesting statements and claims. The first two are certainly credible; but the third can scarcely be true. The weight of human experience over centuries of history is against it. It all depends, of course, on what you mean by *god*. Multitudes of people all down the ages have decided with Nietzsche that 'God is dead' and decided to banish from their minds all belief in the one true God. To some extent they have succeeded, but at a price. For thereafter they have found it practically impossible to live either intellectually or emotionally in a completely god-less world. Deliberately or subconsciously, they have filled the vacuum left by the dismissal of the one true God with all kinds of substitute gods.

Even the stoutest atheist cannot avoid considering what powers brought him and the universe into existence, and what powers will eventually destroy both. He may not call them 'gods', but he might as well; for they are the powers that ultimately control him, and not he them. The atheist dismisses the idea of a personal Creator, and concludes that mindless, impersonal, blind matter and forces are responsible for his existence and for that of the universe. He thus destroys at one stroke all hope of there being any purpose behind his existence. But then he finds that he cannot just exist without some purpose to live for, without any thing bigger than himself to believe in, without any supreme values to honour, and without any cause to devote himself to, and, if need be, sacrifice for. Since he cannot live for and serve the one true God, he invents other lesser purposes and goals, some large and noble and some small and very ignoble. He does not call them 'gods' but he might as well: it comes to the same thing in the end.

Over the course of history, people have made a goddess out of sex (the Greeks called her Aphrodite), a god of alcohol (the Greeks called him Dionysus or Bacchus), a god of war (the Greeks called him Ares, and the Romans called him Mars), a god of money, of pleasure, of fame, a god of the State or even a god of themselves (as many totalitarian dictators have done). Faced with the seemingly unaccountable vicissitudes of life, the atheist man-in-the-street mostly decides that everything is ruled by chance and when he buys a lottery ticket he hopes that Chance will smile on him. Many ancient Greeks thought the same and made a goddess out of it and called her Tyche. And both ancient and modern evolutionists hold that chance is ultimately responsible for the appearance of human beings on earth. Others take the opposite view, that human beings are predetermined machines, and that free will is an illusion. The ancient world had a name for that too. They called it Fate, and made a god of that as well.

Centuries of experience have thus shown that the question is not whether you will believe in God or not, but whether you will believe in the one true God who claims to have made you or in one or many of these other things which you have made into substitute gods.

We shall begin, then, by studying what the Bible means when it talks of the holiness of the one true God. Even an atheist could find it instructive to compare his character and qualities with those of the substitute deities.

Sin

Of course, once admit the possibility that we humans have been created by a personal holy God, then it will not be long before the question of *sin* forces itself into the conversation. Now all healthy-minded people are against crime, and feel strongly that it should be dealt with justly and very firmly; hence prisons and psychiatric institutions. But criminals form no more than a small percentage of the total population. Far more significant is the fact that every single member of the population is to a lesser or greater degree, and at some time or other, morally defective. Not one single person on the face of the earth is morally perfect. Criminals certainly cause a lot of damage and distress. But the average person suffers far more misery from the selfishness, bad temper and unreasonableness that make even his best friends difficult to live with sometimes; from the unfaithfulness, spite, mental cruelty, physical violence that break up the family, lead to divorce, and traumatize the children. And it is the plain lesson of history that in many countries and over many centuries the populace has suffered far more from the broken promises of politicians, the false philosophies and oppression of the governing classes than they have from the criminals whom those governments have thrown into prison.

How has it come about, then, that we are all, without exception, morally defective? Shall we put it down altogether to our genes, say that we can't help it, shuffle off all responsibility for our behaviour, and turn ourselves into mere machines? This much is certain: unless we can arrive at an adequate and true diagnosis of what is morally wrong with us human beings, we shall have no realistic hope of improvement, let alone of cure.

We shall, therefore, be studying the Bible's diagnosis of what is wrong with man. *Sin* is the general term it uses to denote the root cause of the disease itself and also its diverse ramifications. But the general term 'sin' includes several elements which the Bible denotes by special terms and the symptoms which they produce in individuals are likewise variously named. We shall, therefore, study both the root cause and the symptoms, so that then we may be in a position to judge how realistic is the scheme which the Bible proposes in order to deal with them.

Salvation

The Bible's general term for that scheme is, of course, *salvation*. But this is a term which will require careful and detailed study; for it is no exaggeration to say that the popular idea of what the New Testament means by 'salvation' is, in crucial respects, the very opposite of what it does in fact mean.

The popular view of salvation reduces it to an exhortation to live a decently moral life, and daily to improve one's behaviour, driven to it by an uncertain hope of heaven coupled with a fear of more likely ending in hell. The trouble with it is that to many people it seems self-evidently right. If ever you are going to heaven, they argue, it is obvious that you will have to be good. If you are not good, you will obviously not get to heaven. And so deeply rooted is this idea in their minds that they feel no need to read the New Testament to find out what it says. They simply presume that it will say what they expect it to say.

But the fact is that the New Testament teaches the direct opposite of this popular view. Its term 'salvation' is not simply another name for a moral code which we have to keep to earn acceptance with God and a place in his heaven. 'Salvation' means exactly what it says. Its face value is its true value. It is a rescue operation which God effects for those who could never save themselves, try how they will. It is not advice on how to do sufficiently good works to qualify for heaven. The New Testament openly and repeatedly declares that salvation is not by our works: it is the gift of God to those who could never pay for, or deserve, it.

Salvation unfolded

This accounts for the words which the New Testament uses (and which we shall later study) to describe the various elements in salvation. *Ransom* is one of them, and it denotes the price that God has already paid—not which we have to pay—in order to release us from moral and spiritual bondage and set us free. *Justification* is another. It, too, is by God's grace and not by our works or merit. And its effect is to put us in the right with God and to give us peace with him here and now.

So, far from having to live our lives in uncertainty as to whether after death we shall be accepted by God or not, a *justified* person can live his life in the joyous confidence that he has already been accepted by God. And the term *reconciliation*, which we shall also study, will emphasize this fact. What Christ has done is to effect a complete reconciliation between God and man, so that here and now in this life we can be admitted into peace and fellowship with God.

This brings us, here and now, into the possession and enjoyment of *eternal life*. For, contrary to popular opinion, 'eternal life' is not a life into which people enter only after death. It is a life which we can enter into and enjoy here in this world, and need to enter into now, or else we shall never enter into it in the world to come.

But many people, when they first hear someone outline the New Testament's doctrine of salvation in this way, feel it is obviously wrong, if not absurd. In the first place, they say, it undercuts all honest effort at self-improvement, if salvation is not a reward for work well done, but simply a gift given to people irrespective of whether they have done good or bad, merely because they claim to believe. Indeed, they argue, if a person could be absolutely sure that he was already saved 'by faith and not by works', that would mean that he could live the rest of his life in a morally irresponsible way, and still be saved at the end of it, which is moral nonsense.

Now these objections admittedly have a certain superficial force; but they rest on a misconception and they vanish when one opens the New Testament and studies what it actually says. There is no book on earth that insists on holiness more than the New Testament does. Our study of 'holiness' will, therefore, aim to discover what the New Testament means by this term; what it regards as the only acceptable motivation for being holy (which is why, incidentally it maintains that salvation must be a gift and not a payment for being holy); and what power it offers to people so that living a life of genuine goodness becomes a realistic possibility.

Salvation's conditions

This power, the New Testament says, is available on two conditions, the first of which is *repentance*. The meaning of that term might seem to be obvious. We shall find, however, that in the New Testament the term often carries a far more radical meaning than it does in everyday speech.

The second condition is *faith*. But this, many people feel, is the fatally weak point of Christianity. 'Religion', they say, 'all depends on faith, whereas science deals with facts. Science therefore has a solid basis. It can be proved true. Christianity cannot be proved true, and therefore has no reliable basis at all.'

But such people forget that science itself depends fundamentally on faith, and that many of its current theories and interpretations of the universe are based not on proven fact but on the scientists' philosophical presuppositions. They forget also that all personal relationships have to be based in the end on faith. Since the God of the Bible is personal and not an impersonal force, our relationship with him must necessarily and rightly be based on faith. The real question is: What does the New Testament mean by 'faith'? One thing we shall most certainly find is that it does not mean believing something blindly without any evidence. The Bible offers abundant evidence on which to base our faith.

Final judgment

And finally, we shall investigate what the Bible means by *the second death*. It refers to what in popular parlance is called hell. Now for many people the word 'hell' conjures up pictures of demons forking people down into a furnace, and they dismiss the whole concept as primitive superstition. Needless to say, this concept is light-years removed from what the New Testament means by 'the second death'. Of course, the Bible positively teaches that God must punish sin, not only because he is uncompromisingly holy and just, but also because he is unfalteringly love. No morally responsible person in a civilized society holds that crime should be allowed to go on unrestricted and unpunished. God holds the same view about sin.

In these chapters we shall not normally be citing long passages of the Bible but shall give references. We should like to suggest that it would be good to look up each passage, read it aloud and see how it supports the points made in the book.

CHAPTER 2

Holiness

God's Majesty, Purity, Beauty and Love

There is no denying that to many people the very thought of God is unwelcome and any reminder of his holiness a threat. God to them is some grim, almighty tyrant determined to restrict man's freedom and to deny him life's full-blooded pleasures. So they tell themselves that the idea of God is a hangover from man's pre-scientific days, and they try to banish him from their minds (but never with complete success).

All this, however, is in striking contrast to the way people feel and think about God in the Bible. They describe God as their exceeding joy (Ps 43:4); and they enthusiastically make known what they call his virtues. Of course they speak of fearing God, in the sense of reverencing him, of standing in awe of him. But such feelings and emotions are not the cowering, abject reaction of frightened slaves, but the healthy response of intelligent creatures faced with the majesty, power, and purity of their almighty Creator. Even atheistic scientists are sometimes overawed at the vastness, complexity, and sheer beauty of the universe. And what parents have never been amazed and overawed at the perfection of their new-born baby's tiny fingers, complete with miniature finger-nails! It is not surprising, therefore, to find men and women in the Bible calling on each other enthusiastically to worship the Lord in the beauty of holiness (see 1 Chr 16:29).

God's relationship to his creation

God's holiness, then, is in the first instance a way of describing the Creator's relation to the created universe and to all his creatures, human beings included. It indicates that:

1. God stands distinct and separate from the universe. He is not part of its basic material. He is not one of its forces: he is not even the greatest of those forces. He created them: no one or thing created him. He existed before and independently of them. 'He is before all things, and in him all things hold together' (Col 1:17). He upholds, maintains, and controls the universe: no one upholds him (see Isa 46:1–7). He is not the highest God in a hierarchy of angels (though pagans have sometimes talked of him in this way). They are not in the same category as he. They are creatures; he is the Creator. 'There is none holy like the LORD: there is none besides you' (1 Sam 2:2).

2. God is the sole creator of the universe. He did not, as some religions have suggested, delegate the creation of the universe and of mankind to some inferior god or

agent. The Word, by whom all things were made, and without whom nothing was made, was himself God (John 1:1–3). Matter and man are not some second-rate products of some second-rate deity. They have the dignity of having been created by the deliberate act of the all-holy, sole Creator of all things. 'Thus says the LORD, the Holy One of Israel . . . I made the earth and created man on it; it was my hands that stretched out the heavens and I commanded all their host. . . . For thus says the LORD, who created the heavens (he is God!), . . . "I am the LORD, and there is no other"' (Isa 45:11, 12, 18).

3. As man's Creator, God has the sole right to the worship of man's heart. Man was not only made by God, he was made for God. 'Day and night they never cease to say, "Holy, holy, holy is the Lord God Almighty, who was and is and is to come!" . . . "Worthy are you, our Lord and God, to receive glory and honour and power; for you created all things, and by your will they existed and were created."' (Rev 4:8, 11). 'You shall worship the Lord your God and him only shall you serve' (Matt 4:10, citing Deut 6:13).

Herein lies man's dignity and glory. Human life and work are not ultimately pointless and absurd as the existential philosophers have taught. Doing the Creator's will gives man the only goal that is ultimately big enough to satisfy his intellect, emotions, and endeavour.

Herein also lies man's freedom. To worship anyone, or anything, other than God always demeans and enslaves man's spirit in the end. The early Christians were eventually faced with a totalitarian government that demanded that they worship the head of state. But the apostles taught them not to be afraid of the government but to sanctify Christ as Lord in their hearts (1 Pet 3:14–15). That is, in their heart of hearts they must always maintain an awareness of the holiness of the Son of God, of his sole right to be worshipped. And in their remembrance of his holiness they found the courage to refuse the idolatrous demands of their totalitarian government, and thus, at the cost of their lives, to champion the cause of freedom for the human spirit.

The light of God's holiness

To call God holy is also a way of referring to God's absolute and awesome purity. 'The Lord is upright . . . and there is no unrighteousness in him', says the Old Testament (Ps 92:15). 'God is light,' says the New Testament, 'and in him is no darkness at all' (1 John 1:5), not intellectually, nor morally, nor spiritually. In the physical realm it is physical light that gives colour to things. And in the intellectual, moral, and spiritual realms it is the light of God's holiness that brings out the full beauty and meaning of life. Sin does the opposite: it dulls life's colours, deadens its sensibilities, darkens the mind, and blinds the spirit.

On the other hand the light of God's holiness exposes sin. And not only exposes it; for God's holiness is not simply a passive quality, like a frozen pillar of pure white snow. It actively expresses itself in executing his righteous indignation and judgment on human sin. Sometimes this judgment reveals itself in the way in which God has made nature's laws to work. If men persist in sexual perversion, for instance, they find that nature itself turns round and destroys their bodies: 'receiving in themselves the due penalty for their error' (Rom 1:27). At other times, God allows economic and political disaster to overtake those who have rebelled against him. And when he does that, the Bible says that 'the Holy God shows himself holy in righteousness' (Isa 5:16) by judging sin righteously.

In the days of the prophet Isaiah, his nation was guilty of injustice and violence, of ruthless commercial racketeering, of drunken self-indulgence, of deliberate perversions of morality, of complete disregard and defiance of God. Isaiah, therefore, not only denounced their sin: he warned them that God would demonstrate his holiness by bringing down his judgments upon them and reducing the nation to ruin economically, socially, and politically:

> Man is humbled, and each one is brought low, and the eyes of the haughty are brought low. But the LORD of hosts is exalted in justice, and the Holy God shows himself holy in righteousness. . . . for they have rejected the law of the LORD of hosts, and have despised the word of the Holy One of Israel. (see Isa 5:7-30 5:15-16, 24)

But we must come nearer home. God's holiness not only denounces outrageous sinners. Seen in its light, the very best of us appear as sinful. When that same Isaiah was given a vision of God, surrounded by the angelic hosts crying incessantly, 'Holy, holy, holy is the LORD of hosts; the whole earth is full of his glory' (Isa 6:3), Isaiah himself was overwhelmed with an acute sense of his own personal sinfulness and cried out, 'Woe is me! For I am lost; for I am a man of unclean lips, and I dwell in the midst of a people of unclean lips; for my eyes have seen the King, the Lord of hosts!' (Isa 6:5). That is how everyone of us would feel if we became aware of the reality of God's holiness. Lying, hypocrisy, deceit, smutty talk, slander, backbiting, sarcasm, boasting, along with all other sins would suddenly stand exposed as the corrupt and ugly things that they actually are. And we should become painfully aware that such corruption could never be allowed to enter and contaminate the truth and beauty of God's heaven.

But precisely at this point we meet an extraordinary paradox. People in the Bible who have experienced the pain of being exposed by the light of God's holiness suddenly begin to talk enthusiastically about God's light being marvellous. Here is a typical passage: 'But you are a chosen race, a royal priesthood, a holy nation, a people for his own possession, that you may proclaim the excellencies of him who called you out of darkness into his marvellous light. Once you were not a people, but now you are God's people; once you had not received mercy, but now you have received mercy' (1 Pet 2:9-10). Obviously these people have discovered that God's holiness is not simply a negative power. It is a positive power that by its love and mercy can purify sinners and turn them into saints.

God's holy love and its destructive opponents

In Leviticus 19, God first commands his people, 'You shall be holy, for I the Lord your God am holy' (v. 2). He then explains to them in great detail what being holy will mean in practical terms. And one of those terms is this: 'You shall love your neighbour as yourself: I am the Lord' (v. 18).

Holiness then means loving; and God who is supremely holy, is supremely loving, for God is love (1 John 4:16). That same feature of the holiness of God appears in the declaration of God's holy and awesome name in the Bible (see Exod 34:5-7).

We end this chapter, therefore, by pointing out that philosophies which infringe the holiness of the Creator inevitably damage man himself:

Atheism: Refusing to acknowledge the Creator, atheists are obliged to regard the blind impersonal forces of nature as the ultimate powers that unknowingly have created, now control, and will eventually destroy intelligent, moral human beings. Man is thus the prisoner of the material forces of the universe. His intelligence is devalued. He is deprived of any reason and purpose for his existence and robbed of any ultimate hope and goal.

Pantheism: Pantheism identifies God with creation. It teaches that the universe is God, earth is God, the sun is God, man is God, animals are God, everything is God. But if everything is God, then moral evil as well as moral good is God. And this is false. When God created the world, he saw that everything he made was good (Gen 1:31). God is not to be identified with moral evil. He is holy. And in this fact lies the certain hope that one day evil will be overcome.

If evil were God, as pantheism teaches, there would be no hope that evil would ever be overcome. Pantheism is not only false: it is, in spite of its superficial attractiveness, the worst form of pessimism.

Various forms of reincarnationism: Some religions and religious philosophies hold that matter is essentially bad.

They teach that the supreme God would never have created matter. What he did, so they say, was to create lesser gods, who like him had creatorial powers. They in turn created still lesser gods, and eventually one of these gods very unwisely created the material universe and human beings. Human beings are thus an unfortunate mixture of soul (which is good) and matter (which is bad). Matter infects and defiles the soul, drags it down into evil behaviour which in turn involves the person in inevitable suffering. If this suffering has not been exhausted by the time the person comes to die, the soul is doomed to be reincarnated in another material body. Then, if in this life it is guilty of further evil behaviour, it is doomed to yet further suffering and re-incarnations. The only hope is that somehow or other the soul may exhaust all the suffering, keep absolutely clear of further sin, and so return to the pure World-Soul and escape all further re-incarnation in material bodies.

This doctrine is a double infringement of the holiness of God: (a) There is in fact only one Creator, not a multiplicity of lesser creators; (b) Matter is not essentially bad, but essentially good, as we have seen. Man's trouble does not spring from the fact that he has a material body, but from his sinful abuse of his free will and from his disobedience to God.

In addition, this doctrine is not only false, it is very cruel. It teaches that if a child is born with a disability, this is the result of sins done in previous incarnations. If, after all these (possibly) thousands of reincarnations, the child has still not exhausted the suffering of past sins, what hope has the child of working off the suffering in this present life—let alone the possibility that he will commit further sins in this life and so add to the inevitable need for further re-incarnations?

This doctrine, then, is a monstrosity of untruth and cruelty. Man is not saved by his own sufferings but by the sufferings of Christ:

> But he was wounded for our transgressions; he was crushed for our iniquities; upon him was the chastisement that brought us peace, and with his stripes we are healed. (Isa 53:5)

Nor need people live out their lives in fear of an array of lesser, irresponsible, and sometimes malevolent deities. There is only one God, and that God loves us and offers himself as our Saviour:

> They have no knowledge who . . . keep on praying to a god that cannot save. . . . And there is no other god besides me, a righteous God and a Saviour; there is none besides me. Turn to me and be saved, all the ends of the earth! For I am God, and there is no other. (Isa 45:20–22)

> For I am the Lord your God, the Holy One of Israel, your Saviour. . . . the God of the whole earth he is called. (Isa 43:3; 54:5)

CHAPTER 3

Sin

A Disease, Its Symptoms and Its Cure

One does not necessarily have to live very long to discover that there is something wrong with people. Some unfortunate children discover it all too soon, when parents, whom they had a right to expect to be always kind and loving, act unreasonably, lose their tempers and mistreat them. They will later discover that this 'something wrong' is not confined to their parents and family: in differing forms, and in greater or lesser degree, there is something wrong with everybody.

History shows that this 'something wrong' has been endemic in international relationships in all ages without exception; and still today, in spite of huge, beneficial advancements in every kind of science and technology, it reveals itself in monstrously irrational behaviour. If only the nations could trust each other and cooperate instead of competing in the development of earth's resources, they could turn the world into a paradise. Deserts could be made fruitful; poverty, famine, and epidemics eliminated; and everybody's welfare and lifespan increased. But no, nations do not, and cannot, trust each other; and in consequence oceans of money, time, and energy are spent on ever more sophisticated weapons of destruction.

But it is not only nations that behave irrationally. We all do. You do, I do. Sooner or later, in spite of all our resolutions and good intentions we have to admit, as Paul put it centuries ago, 'For I do not do the good I want, but the evil I do not want is what I keep on doing' (Rom 7:19).

What then is wrong with us? What is this universal disease from which we all suffer? The ancient Greek tragedians, Aeschylus, Sophocles, and Euripides, studied its symptoms and tried to probe its causes. So did the ancient philosophers, and so do modern ones. And so have literary giants from every continent. It is certain that we shall never truly understand ourselves or the world we live in, unless we face this disease realistically. The Bible confidently and joyously insists that we can find continuing and increasing deliverance from it; and it calls this deliverance *salvation*. But we shall not grasp what salvation means, or how it works, unless we first understand the biblical term for the disease.

That term is 'sin'. To help us understand it, let us use the analogy of physical disease. Medical personnel must distinguish between the symptoms of the disease itself and the root cause of the disease. For if one is going to achieve a cure, it is no good just suppressing the symptoms without getting rid of the disease. And there is no hope of that unless one can attack the root-cause and eliminate it.

Take jaundice, for example, which, strictly speaking, is not a disease but an outward symptom of some internal disorder, such as gallstones, or a cancer of the pancreas, etc. Clearly, it would be no use trying to get rid of the jaundice, if one did not get at the underlying cause.

Specific symptoms of sin

The New Testament gives us various lists of the symptoms of sin, and normally adds a warning about the gravity of these symptoms. Here is one list:

> Now the works of the flesh are evident: sexual immorality, impurity, sensuality, idolatry, sorcery, enmity, strife, jealousy, fits of anger, rivalries, dissensions, divisions, envy, drunkenness, orgies, and things like these. I warn you, as I warned you before, that those who do such things will not inherit the kingdom of God. (Gal 5:19–21)

Here is another, which gives a gruesome description of the symptoms that can occur when the disease of sin is in an advanced stage:

> as it is written: 'None is righteous, no, not one; no one understands; no one seeks for God. All have turned aside; together they have become worthless; no one does good, not even one.'

> 'Their throat is an open grave; they use their tongues to deceive.'

'The venom of asps is under their lips.'

'Their mouth is full of curses and bitterness.'

'Their feet are swift to shed blood; in their paths are ruin and misery, and the way of peace they have not known.'

'There is no fear of God before their eyes.' (Rom 3:10–18)

None of these lists implies, of course, that all the symptoms are to be found in equal proportions in everybody. On the other hand, the New Testament insists that everybody shows some symptoms, for the disease is universal.

General symptoms of sin

Then there are what may be called more general symptoms. One of these is *moral weakness*. 'For while we were still weak . . .' (Rom 5:6).

As an example we may take Pontius Pilate, the Roman governor, who was responsible for the crucifixion of Jesus Christ (Matt 27:11–26; Luke 23:1–25; John 18:28–19:16). He was the last man you would have suspected of being weak. He was a high-ranking soldier, the officer in command of the Roman army in Judaea; and he was also responsible for law and order in the country.

Outwardly, Pilate was like a great beam of wood that on the surface looks solid and strong, but inside it has been eaten away by wood-worm; and when you put pressure on it, it collapses.

When he talked with Jesus in private, and became aware of the reality of God and of the enormous sin it would be if he crucified the innocent Son of God, he decided he must do what he knew to be right and release Jesus (John 19:8–12). But when he went outside, the crowd shouted menacingly and their leaders blackmailed him, threatening to slander him to the Roman emperor. And Pilate caved in. Though he knew that what he was about to do was a criminal betrayal of justice, fear destroyed his resistance and out of fear he sentenced Jesus to be crucified.

This leads us to ask: have we never told a lie out of fear of what the consequences would be if we told the truth? Have we never done something that we knew to be wrong, because the group to which we belonged insisted on doing it, and we were afraid to stand against the group?

Another general symptom of sin is *ungodliness*:

> understanding this, that the law is not laid down for the just but for the lawless and disobedient, for the ungodly and sinners, for the unholy and profane, for those who strike their fathers and mothers, for murderers, the sexually immoral, men who practise homosexuality, enslavers, liars, perjurers, and what-ever else is contrary to sound doctrine, in accordance with the gospel of the glory of the blessed God with which I have been entrusted. (1 Tim 1:9–11)

The original Greek word here translated 'ungodly' means 'people who have no respect or reverence'. The one for whom they have no respect or reverence is, in the first place, God. But it does not stop there. Man is made in the image of God; and when people lose respect and reverence for the Creator, they begin to devalue his creature, man. They lose respect for the sanctity of the human body—their own and other people's. This spawns the large and ugly brood of sexual sins, abuse of alcohol and drugs which injure physical health and enfeeble the mind. They lose respect for the sanctity of truth. Hence all kinds of lies, deceptions, and broken promises. In the end, they lose respect for the sanctity of life. Hence the endless crimes of violence.

Alienation and Enmity against God is another symptom: 'the mind of the flesh is enmity against God' (Rom 8:7 RV); 'and you, being in time past alienated and enemies in your mind in your evil works' (Col 1:21 RV).

Large-scale examples of this particular symptom have been all too evident throughout the past century and right up to the present day. The governments in many countries have used all their power in an attempt to systematically blot out all belief in God and Christ. But enmity against God is not confined to outright atheists. Sometimes, even outwardly religious people can at heart be enemies of God. The Christian apostle, Paul, was always very religious; but he was a bitter enemy of Jesus Christ before he was converted (1 Tim 1:12-17).

The fact is that there is a rebel against God in the heart of every one of us. When God commands us in the Bible to do something or not to do something, his very command often stirs up resentment inside us and makes us want to do the very opposite. The Apostle Paul cites an example from his own experience (Rom 7:5, 7-9). For some years he lived unaware of God's commandment 'You shall not covet'. But then God brought this command home to his heart; and Paul found that this very commandment stirred up all kinds of coveting in his heart that, struggle as he might, he could not control—and what is more, deep down within him, did not altogether want to control.

Of course, this basic enmity against God does not necessarily, or often, express itself as open hostility to God. More often it takes the form of indifference.

Now if someone says, 'I'm just not interested in music or art', we may think it is a pity; but we do not get upset about it, for it is only a matter of taste. But if a woman says 'I'm just not interested in my husband', it is tragic; for it is clear evidence that she is alienated from her husband. Love has been destroyed. And if someone says, 'I'm just not interested in God', this is supremely tragic. We owe our very existence to God. Not to be interested in him is an unmistakable symptom that, somewhere along the line, serious alienation from God has taken place.

These, then, are some of the symptoms. But the underlying disease involves *a desire to be independent of God* our Creator. According to the Bible (Gen 3), the very first sin which mankind committed was not something crude and lurid like murder or immorality. It occurred when Adam and Eve were tempted by the devil to grasp at independence of God so as to decide by themselves what was good and what was evil. They imagined that they could safely be their own god. So they took the forbidden fruit. It led at once to alienation from God and a sense of guilt and shame which made them want to run away and hide from God, whom they now felt to be against them.

We have all followed them down that path of disobedience and independence. But to live like that is to live an untruth, an unreality. We did not create ourselves. We are creatures of God. To live alienated and independent of him is contrary to the fundamental law of our existence.

And so the New Testament says that *sin is lawlessness*:

> Everyone who makes a practice of sinning also practises lawlessness; sin is lawlessness. (1 John 3:4)

Now we know what dangers we would run if we disregarded the Creator's physical laws, like, for example, the laws of electricity. Suppose a man buys an electric light but makes no attempt to read or follow the manufacturer's instructions. He wires it up as he himself thinks best. As a result he electrocutes himself. We should scarcely pity him: we should call him a fool for neglecting the maker's instructions and taking no notice of the laws of electricity. Similarly, fundamental neglect of, and disobedience to, the Creator's moral and spiritual laws must lead to moral and spiritual disaster. It is the root cause of all sin's many symptoms.

The remarkable thing is that, according to the Bible, there is a cure. 'The saying is trustworthy and deserving of full acceptance, that Christ Jesus came into the world to save sinners' (1 Tim 1:15). 'For God did not send his Son into the world to condemn the world, but in order that the world might be saved through him.' (John 3:17). The following chapters, therefore, will study the terms which the New Testament uses to describe this salvation and how it works.

But there are two things we should notice at once. Many people think that the way to be saved is to do our best to cut out the symptoms of sin from our lives. That is a good enough thing in itself to do; but it cannot save us. You may cut every apple off an apple tree; but the tree is still an apple tree. That is its inward nature. So even if we could suppress every symptom of sin, we should still have a sinful nature within us. And that, says the New Testament, is not our fault. We were born that way. We inherited a fallen sinful nature from our first parent, Adam. But in a similar way we can, if we will, receive from Christ his unfallen, holy life, the nature of which is to live a life pleasing to God. 'For through one man's [Adam's] disobedience the many were made sinners, so through the obedience of the one [Christ] shall the many be made righteous' (Rom 5:19 own trans.).

And the second thing to notice is this: God loves us while we are still sinners. This is the secret why God's salvation is so practical and actually works. We do not have to improve ourselves before God is prepared to accept us and begin his great work of salvation within us. He loves us and is prepared to accept us as we are. This is the burden of the argument in Romans 5:6–11, a passage any person who is serious about the problem of sin should think through rigorously.

CHAPTER 4

Reconciliation

The Way to Peace

In our last chapter we studied the moral and spiritual disease from which we all suffer and its symptoms of alienation from our Creator. Now we begin to examine the terms which describe the cure.

First comes the delightful word *reconciliation* together with its cognate verb, 'to reconcile'. It is perhaps the easiest of all our terms to understand because we already know what it means in our relationships with other people. Most of us at some time in life have gone through some such experience as the following. We have done, or said, something wrong that has deeply hurt, or even injured, some friend or other. Eventually the friend has faced us with our wrongdoing. But instead of admitting it, and asking for forgiveness, pride or fear has made us deny our fault, or even lie about it; and we have got angry, and made a lot of counter-accusations against him.

And then we have gone off, muttering 'I never want to talk to him or see him again.' With that there has begun a long period of alienation, distance, and silence. During that time, if anyone should happen innocently to praise our former friend, we have resented it. And then we have put forward our (distorted) side of the story, to blacken our former friend's character, and so justify our animosity towards him.

It is like that with many people in their relationship with God. Memory and a bad conscience make them aware deep inside that if there is a Creator, he must be against their sins and, so they imagine, against them as well. Instead of admitting their sins, therefore, they deny there is a Creator. If they should meet somebody who believes in God, who loves and worships him, they inwardly resent it and accuse God of all the evils that religious people have committed as if that were God's fault (and as if atheists had never committed any evil), or else they blame God for allowing so much suffering in the world, and so on. And so their alienation from their Creator persists, and life remains grey with the dark shadow of ultimate purposelessness and hopelessness, lit up only by the fitful protests of a bad conscience that refuses permanently to lie down and be quiet.

The first move

Reconciliation is the word that tells us that God himself has acted to overcome this alienation, to dispel the misunderstandings on which it is based, and to remove the obstacles to peace. There are two passages from the New Testament that tell us how:

He [Jesus Christ] is the image of the invisible God, the firstborn of all creation. For by him all things were created, in heaven and on earth, visible and invisible, whether thrones or dominions or rulers or authorities—all things were created through him and for him. And he is before all things, and in him all things hold together. And he is the head of the body, the church. He is the beginning, the firstborn from the dead, that in everything he might be pre-eminent. For in him all the fullness of God was pleased to dwell, and through him to reconcile to himself all things, whether on earth or in heaven, making peace by the blood of his cross.

And you, who once were alienated and hostile in mind, doing evil deeds, he has now reconciled in his body of flesh by his death, in order to present you holy and blameless and above reproach before him. (Col 1:15–22)

You can find the second passage in 2 Corinthians 5:18–21. The first thing to notice in what these passages say about reconciliation is that in this process *God has made the first move*:

For in him [that is in Christ] it was decreed that all the fullness should dwell and that through him [God] should reconcile all things to himself. For in Christ God was reconciling the world to himself. (own trans.)

Now this is remarkable, for God's normal rule for human beings when they fall out among themselves is that it is the responsibility of the one that did the wrong to take the initiative in effecting a reconciliation. 'So,' said Christ, 'if you are offering your gift at the altar and there remember that your brother has something against you, leave your gift there before the altar and go. First be reconciled to your brother, and then come and offer your gift' (Matt 5:23-24). But God had done the world no wrong. He had nothing to apologize for. It was human beings that had started all the enmity by rebelling against him. Nonetheless it is God who has made the first move towards our being reconciled with him, by sending his Son into the world.

And this is remarkable for another reason. Often, when two human beings have fallen out, they wish they could make a move towards being friends again. But each is afraid of being rebuffed by the other party. But God sent his Son into the world knowing in advance that he would be rejected, humiliated, and crucified. Indeed that is why the Son of God, through whom the universe was made, came among us with his divine glory veiled in human form. His unveiled glory would have made it impossible for them to approach him, let alone express their hostility to him. As it was, they vented all their hostility against God on Jesus Christ and put him to a cross. And when they had done that, God had it announced that he loved them still and was prepared to forgive them for that and for all their other sins (Acts 2:36-39). For he loved them even while they were still enemies.

Here then was God's answer to the slander that the devil had insinuated into the thinking of the human race, that God is a tyrant and waiting only for the first opportunity to prevent humans from expressing their personalities to the full and from pursuing their own healthy ambitions (Gen 3).

It was not that God had gone soft on sin, and was prepared to capitulate to human arrogance and wickedness in order to retain or regain man's friendship. The Almighty is no pushover. He could not and would not take the view that man's sin did not matter. We need, therefore, to understand what the New Testament means by the term 'reconcile' when it says, 'By Christ God was reconciling the world to himself.' And to do that we need to consider the way the word was used in ancient Greek, the language in which the New Testament was written.

If a man A had by his wrongdoing deeply offended another man B, then B had every right to be angry with A, and to hold his wrongdoing against him. To reconcile A to B, therefore, you had not so much to change A's idea of B, but to remove the cause of B's just anger against A.

Now God's anger against sin is not some temporary loss of temper that causes him to act out of character. Nor is it a feeling of indignation that eventually fades away. Nor can it be a private sense of displeasure which he keeps locked up secretly in his head. Sin is a challenge to the very being and character of God; and as the moral governor of the universe, God must openly and actively express the indignation of his whole being against it. It means, therefore, that he cannot permanently overlook sin, still less act as if it did not matter. Not until sin is punished, and that publicly before the eyes of the whole universe, can God's indignation be assuaged and his character vindicated. To reconcile the world to himself, therefore, God had first to remove the cause of his indignation against the world: he had to punish the world's sin. There could be no reconciliation, no welcoming back of men and women into his friendship without it.

And that is why, by the united decree of the Godhead, the Son of God became human without ceasing to be God. Since all the fullness of the Godhead dwelled in him, he could represent God to men. What men did to him, they did to God. How he reacted to men, is how God reacted. In him men could see what God was really like.

At the same time because he was genuinely human (though not merely human) he could stand as the representative of the human race before God. He thus could, and did, take on himself, as mankind's representative and substitute, the sin of the world, and could publicly bear the indignation of God and suffer sin's punishment. He thus removed completely the cause of God's indignation against the world and made it possible for man to be reconciled to God and be at peace with him.

We read in 2 Corinthians 5:19–21,

> in Christ God was reconciling the world to himself, not counting their trespasses against them, . . . For our sake he made him [Jesus Christ] to be sin who knew no sin, so that in him we might become the righteousness of God.

That is to say, when Christ, though sinless himself, took on himself the sin of the world as mankind's representative, God treated him as if the world's sins were his. The just punishment of mankind's sins was thus endured by Christ and exhausted, with the result that there remains no obstacle in the way of man's return to God. Justice no longer obliges God to impute the world's sins to them. All may come to God through Christ, be reconciled to him, and be at peace with him now and forever. Man does not have to make his own peace with God. Christ has already done that for him. All man needs to do is to accept the reconciliation and peace that Christ has made. So coming to God, he finds himself accepted as if he were Christ himself, or, to put it as the Bible puts it, he is regarded as being as perfectly right with God as Christ is ('to become the righteousness of God in him').

Does this mean, then, that all men everywhere are saved, or ultimately will be, whether they carry on ignoring God and leading sinful lives, or not, even whether they remain atheists or not? No, of course not. Christ has certainly made reconciliation and peace with God for all mankind. But the question remains whether we on our side are willing to accept the peace or not. It has sometimes happened in history when the leaders of two warring nations have called a truce and then have signed a peace treaty, that a breakaway group in one of the nations has refused to accept the peace. It has continued to regard the other nation as an enemy, and those of its own nation that have accepted the peace, as traitors. And it has gone on fighting.

So is it with us and God. Those who accept the peace that Christ has made are said, in the New Testament, to 'receive the reconciliation' and so to enter into permanent peace with God (Rom 5:1, 11). But it is possible for people to refuse the reconciliation and to continue with their indifference and hostility to their Creator. For a creature to do that must, of course, inevitably lead to disaster.

Relationships and restoration

Two further benefits spring from the peace which Christ has made. The first is this. Those who through Christ have been personally reconciled to God find that it also makes peace between them and all others who have similarly been reconciled to God through Christ.

> Therefore remember that at one time you Gentiles in the flesh, . . . were . . . separated from Christ, alienated from the commonwealth of Israel . . . But now in Christ Jesus you who once were far off have been brought near by the blood of Christ. For he himself is our peace, who has made us both one and has broken down in his flesh the dividing wall of hostility by abolishing the law of commandments expressed in ordinances, that he might create in himself one new man in place of the two, so making peace, and might reconcile us both to God in one body through the cross, thereby killing the hostility. And he came and preached peace to you who were far off and peace to those who were near. For through him we both have access in one Spirit to the Father. (Eph 2:11–18)

This passage describes how Christ puts an end to the age-long animosity between Jews and non-Jews. But the same thing applies to all those other barriers of race, nationalism, social status, and religion, that have produced such deep divisions in the human race. It is, of course, unfortunately true that all too often in the course of history people and nations who have claimed to be Christian have persecuted and fought other people and nations who have likewise claimed to be Christian. But such behaviour casts serious doubt on whether the parties concerned have ever really been reconciled to God. It suggests rather that their profession of Christianity has been merely formal and superficial; that, as the New Testament puts it, they have received 'the grace of God in vain' (2 Cor 6:1).

The second, immense, benefit is this: one day God is going to reconcile the whole universe of intelligent beings to himself (see the quotation from Col 1:20, p. 31). Once more, unfortunately, that does not mean that every being in the universe, the devil included, will become loyal friends of God; for God will not remove any creature's free-will, not even for the purpose of turning rebels into saints. But the situation is this: God is not going to wait forever. One day he is going to restore and redevelop the earth and the universe. That will mean that he will have to restrain by force all who persist in their rebellion against him. But when he does so, none will be able to raise his voice in moral protest. The cross of Christ will silence every objection. All could have been saved by God's magnificent grace at Christ's expense. Not even those who perish will be able to criticize God on moral grounds for it. The universe will have been completely pacified (Rev 5:11–14).

CHAPTER 5

Justification

Getting Things Legally Right

The next two basic terms which the New Testament uses to describe what God is prepared to do for us are *justify* and *justification*. They are legal terms. This upsets some people. They argue that if there is a God at all, he must love us as a father loves his children and will be prepared to welcome back his erring children like the father did his boy in Jesus' famous parable of the Prodigal Son (Luke 15). That father did not act as a judge and drag his repentant son through a law court; nor, so these critics say, will God.

But this is shallow thinking. Even in the parable, while the father forgave the prodigal, and reinstated him as son, he did not take away the elder brother's part of the inheritance and give half of it to the returning prodigal to make up for the fact that the prodigal had squandered his own part! That would have been highly unjust; and God's forgiveness can never be at the expense of justice either towards himself or to other people.

Suppose your daughter worked in a bank. One day a robber entered the bank, shot her, and made off with a large sum of money. What would you think of the judge if he said, when the criminal was brought before him: 'Though this man is a criminal, he is my son and I love him. He says he is sorry. So I am going to forgive him without imposing any penalty'? Would you not protest that such forgiveness was utterly unjust both to you and to your daughter, and that it undercut the whole basis of a just and civilized society? What the parable of the Prodigal Son teaches is certainly true: God is prepared to forgive his children. But that is only one side of the truth. The other side is that God's forgiveness must be, and must be seen to be, consistent with universal justice.

Now we shall presently find that the verb 'to justify' has two basic connotations:

1. To declare someone to be in the right.

2. To demonstrate that someone or something is right.

It does not mean 'to *make* someone right.' Luke 7:29 says that 'all the people . . . justified God.' That cannot mean that the people *made* God righteous. God was never less than righteous; no one had to make him righteous. It means 'the people *declared* that God was righteous.'

But now let's start at the beginning. Here is an example of the use of the word in a human court of justice in biblical times.

> If there arises a controversy between men and they resort to judgment and the judges judge their case; then they shall justify the righteous and condemn the wicked. (Deut 25:1 own trans.)

The meaning of the phrase 'justify the righteous and condemn the wicked' is obvious. 'To condemn the wicked' does not mean 'to make him wicked' but 'to declare him wicked', or, 'in the wrong.' Similarly 'to justify the righteous' means that the man who is finally proven to have behaved justly must be declared to be in the right. Unfortunately, it sometimes happens in human courts that the man who has actually committed the wrong is able to bribe the judge and jury to give a false verdict. The Bible loudly condemns this perversion of justice:

> He who justifies the wicked [that is, declares the wicked man to be in the right] and he who condemns the righteous, are both alike an abomination to the LORD. (Prov 17:15)

With that in mind, read the following parable told by Jesus. It will contain some surprises.

> He also told this parable to some who trusted in themselves that they were righteous, and treated others with contempt: 'Two men went up into the temple to pray, one a Pharisee and the other a tax-collector. The Pharisee, standing by himself, prayed thus: "God, I thank you that I am not like other men, extortioners, unjust, adulterers, or even like this tax-collector. I fast twice a week; I give tithes of all that I get." But the tax-collector, standing far off, would not even lift up his eyes to heaven, but beat his breast, saying, "God, be merciful to me, a sinner!" I tell you, this man went down to his house justified, rather than the other. For

everyone who exalts himself will be humbled, but
the one who humbles himself will be exalted.' (Luke
18:9–14)

The first thing to notice is that here Jesus uses the
term 'justify': 'the tax-collector went home justified'. Now
this is interesting. The Pharisee and the tax-collector had
not gone to an earthly court of law to appear before an
earthly judge. They had gone up into the temple to pray.
But as they stood before God and reviewed their lives,
God acted as their judge and passed his verdict on them.

The second thing to notice is that, according to Christ,
one of the two men went home justified; that is, God as
judge declared this man to be in the right before God's
court.

The third thing to notice is that while the one man
was justified by God, the other man was not. And this
is very startling! For the tax-collector was on his own
admission a sinner; and most people of his times would
have regarded tax collecting for the imperialist Romans,
with all the cheating that it involved, as one of the most
despicable forms of sin. Yet he was the one whom God
justified! The Pharisee, on the other hand, was a man
who tried to live as good a life as he possibly could, reli-
giously, commercially, and socially: he was not unjust, nor
an extortioner, nor an adulterer; he fasted twice a week,
tithed his income and gave it to God for the use of others.
Yet God did not justify him.

At first sight, this is not only startling: it is shocking.
The Bible itself, as we have already seen, forbade earthly
judges to justify the wicked, and condemn the righteous.

How then, when these two men appeared in God's court, could God justify the tax-collector, who was the 'bad man,' and not justify the Pharisee, who was the 'good man'? Part of the answer is to be found in the following principles.

1. The standards of God's law are absolute. God's standards are different from ours. If a boy sits for an exam at school and gets 70 marks out of a hundred, he will probably pass the exam, even though he has come 30 marks short of 100. But God's law is not like that. It demands 100 percent perfection all the time. And none of us has attained to that. Some of us may be better than others. But God is truthful: he cannot pretend that we are better than we are. His verdict is that we 'all have sinned and fall short of the glory [that is, the perfect standards] of God' (Rom 3:23).

2. God's law is a whole. Break one commandment and you are guilty of breaking the whole law, says the Bible (Jas 2:10). Perhaps that sounds unfair at first, but God's law is not a collection of unrelated commands such that if you break only one it leaves all the rest undamaged. God's law is a unified whole. Its aim and demand is perfection. Break one command, and then, even if you kept all the rest, the result would still not be perfection. Break one link in an anchor chain and the ship goes adrift. Make one slip in adding up a long list of figures and you get the whole sum wrong. And even the best of us have broken much more than one of God's commandments.

3. God's law therefore condemns us all. Whether we have tried to do good, like the Pharisee, or have done badly like the tax-collector, we have all broken God's law. And the Bible says: 'Now we know that whatever the law says it speaks to those who are under the law, so that every mouth may be stopped, and the whole world may be held accountable to God' (Rom 3:19).

The answer to one half of our problem

And now we can begin to see the answer to one half, at least, of our problem: Why was the Pharisee not justified? Because, when he came before God, he recited all his good deeds, all his honest efforts to keep God's law; and he hoped on these grounds that God would justify him. But that was impossible. Good though his efforts were, he had still come short, he had broken God's law. He therefore deserved to suffer its penalty. God could not pretend otherwise. His Word says: 'For by works of the law no human being will be justified in his sight, since through the law comes knowledge of sin' (Rom 3:20).

'If that is so,' says someone, 'that must mean that God cannot declare anyone to be right; he can justify nobody that comes before his court. But then what about the tax-collector? He surely had broken God's law worse than the Pharisee. How, then, could Christ say that the tax-collector went home from the temple justified?'

The answer to the other half of our problem

There are theoretically two ways by which we can be justified by God. One way is to keep his law perfectly: God can then pronounce us 'right with God'. But that way is in fact impossible for us, as we have seen. We have all broken his law already.

The other way of being justified is by paying the penalty for breaking God's law. But if we had to do that, it would mean for us eternal separation from God. Hence the predicament we all are in.

God's solution is that his own Son as mankind's representative has paid the penalty for us by bearing the judgment of God against sin and dying on the cross. If, therefore, we put our faith in Jesus, God can count his death as our death; our penalty having thus been paid by Jesus, God can justify us, that is, declare us to be right before his judgment throne.

Here is how the Bible puts it:

> for all have sinned and fall short of the glory of God, and are justified by his grace as a gift, through the redemption that is in Christ Jesus, whom God put forward as a propitiation by his blood, to be received by faith. This was to show God's righteousness, because in his divine forbearance he had passed over former sins. It was to show his righteousness at the present time, so that he might be just and the justifier of the one who has faith in Jesus. (Rom 3:23–26)

Does this mean that all men and women are automatically justified? No. According to the parable once more, the Pharisee was not justified. The tax-collector was, and that because, as he stood before God, he smote his breast and so confessed his sin, condemned himself, and acknowledged that he deserved to suffer the penalty of having broken God's law. Then, in faith, he cast himself on God's mercy saying, 'God, be merciful to me, a sinner.' There and then God justified him, that is, declared him to be right with God, free of the penalty of sin, justified once and for all.

Moreover the Bible tells us that 'It is appointed for man to die once, and after that comes the judgment' (Heb 9:27). That means that God does not summon us before his judgment throne every day of our lives. There is to be only one judgment day; and that comes after we die. At that one judgment, the whole of life will be reviewed, and God's verdict pronounced.

And the wonderful thing is that we do not have to wait until the judgment day before we know what the verdict will be (see also John 5:24). God tells those who put their faith in Christ that Christ's once-for-all death on the cross is sufficient to cover the whole of their lives in view of the one judgment day. They have nothing to fear, therefore. Once justified through faith in Christ, they remain justified forever; and having been justified by faith, they have permanent peace with God (Rom 5:1).

To sum up so far: if we ask, 'On what conditions can we be justified before God?' the answer which the New Testament gives is: 'For we hold that one is justified by faith apart from works of the law' (Rom 3:28). 'Why, then,' says somebody, 'does the New Testament say elsewhere: "You see that a person is justified by works and not by faith alone (Jas 2:24)"? Is this not a contradiction?'

The meaning of justification by works

No, it is not a contradiction. James is using the term 'justify' in its other connotation: not to *declare* someone to be right, but to *prove,* or *demonstrate* someone to be right. It is certainly true that a man is declared to be right with God on the ground of his faith and not of his works. But the only way the man can demonstrate to his family and friends that he has this kind of faith, is by the way he behaves, that is, by his works.

Suppose a man tells his friends: 'Last week I received a letter telling me that a rich relative of mine had died and bequeathed me a very large sum of money. All I needed to do was to go to the bank and claim this free gift. I believed the letter, claimed the gift, and now I am immensely rich.'

Would not his friends have the right to reply: 'You say you are rich through simply believing the letter. But please show us by your changed lifestyle that your faith and the gift are real, not just a story that you have made up. Justify your story by your works.' So those who have been justified by God through faith and not by works must demonstrate their faith was, and is, genuine. There is only one way that you can demonstrate that your faith is genuine, and that is, as James says, by your works.

CHAPTER 6

Ransom and Redemption

The Price of Freedom

In their literal sense, the terms *ransom* and *redemption* were in common use in the ancient world, just as they are in ours. People were kidnapped and held for ransom. Their family and friends would then have to pay a large sum of money for their release. Modern terrorists hijack a plane and threaten to kill the passengers one by one, or else to blow up the whole plane, unless their demands are met. They may not ask for money: their demand might be the release of fellow-terrorists previously caught and imprisoned by the government. In this case, we still use words like 'price', and 'cost', and 'ransom', but now in a metaphorical sense; and we say that the release of the terrorists is the price that the government would have to pay to ransom the plane load of passengers from death, unless they took the risk of storming the plane.

It is important to notice here that you only use the word 'redeem' if you are buying someone out of prison and slavery, or out of the threat of death, into freedom. You would not use the words 'ransom' or 'redeem' to describe the activity of corrupt businessmen who, in some countries, are prepared to pay a lot of money to buy little girls from their poor parents in order to use them as child prostitutes. They would be buying these girls, not to free them from slavery, but to enslave them.

In certain circumstances people can even redeem something that is their own property. A man who urgently needs money may decide to pawn his watch. The pawnbroker will take the watch and give the man an amount of cash. But the watch does not immediately become the property of the pawn-broker. For a certain period of time, the watch, strictly speaking, remains the original man's property. But if he wants to regain actual possession of his property, he must redeem it within that time, that is, buy it back; and the price he will have to pay will, of course, far exceed the amount he originally received from the pawn-broker.

In everyday speech, then, the words 'ransom' and 'redemption' carry several slightly different connotations, some literal, some metaphorical. Similarly in the New Testament, though here, in theological contexts, the terms are always used in a metaphorical sense. There is no thought of any money transaction. 'You were not redeemed with silver or gold', says the Apostle Peter (1 Pet 1:18). But running through all the New Testament usages are the following themes:

1. Buying, or buying back, people from debt, or slavery, or imprisonment or threat of penalty, or death.

2. Always it is God or Christ who is said to do the buying, or redeeming. No human is said to redeem himself or his fellow human.

3. The paying of a price, or ransom. And here again it is only God or Christ who is said to pay the price or bear the cost of the ransom. People are never asked, or allowed, to contribute anything to the price that had to be paid for their redemption. This is in striking contrast to many religions in which people are required to achieve salvation at the cost of their own self-effort or suffering, or even by the payment of money. When the priests and merchants in the temple at Jerusalem gave the people the impression that they could and must pay for salvation, Christ drove them all out (John 2:13–16).

4. The purpose of redemption is always to bring people into freedom and to enrich them with an eternal inheritance.

Freedom from what?

1. Freedom from the guilt of past sins. One cannot undo the past. God himself will not change history. What has been done, has been done. What God offers us through Christ is release from the guilt of past sins. Many people are haunted by the past. Much as they try to forget what has happened, and to start afresh, they cannot shake off the guilt of their previous misdeeds.

Others, with a less-well-functioning conscience, find that they can easily dismiss their past, like the adulteress in the book of Proverbs who 'eats and wipes her mouth and says, "I have done no wrong"' (30:20). But such irresponsibility does not break the chain of real guilt (we are not here thinking about psychological guilt-complexes). Some years ago, robbers in Great Britain assaulted a train, injured the driver for life, and absconded to South America with millions of pounds of money. There they bribed the authorities not to extradite them. Perhaps the robbers felt no guilt over their crime. But that made no difference to the fact that when they set foot in Britain they were immediately prosecuted and imprisoned. One day every man and woman will find themselves in God's court. The mere passage of years, or a conveniently short memory, will not have wiped out the past. Unless they have allowed Christ to remove the guilt that chains them to their past, the chain will remain eternally.

Redemption signifies that God can break those chains for us in this life if we will repent. The act of breaking the chain is called forgiveness. In the original Greek of the New Testament, the most frequent word for forgiveness (*aphesis*) means 'release' or 'discharge.' It is a word that is used of releasing someone from prison, or of discharging a debtor, or of setting a slave free. And the cost of this release is paid by Christ: 'we have redemption', says the New Testament, 'through his blood, the forgiveness of our trespasses [sins]' (Eph 1:7). Thus the chain is broken never to be replaced. The redemption Christ has paid for is an eternal redemption (Heb 9:11–12).

2. *Freedom from the curse pronounced by God's law.* 'Christ redeemed us from the curse of the law by becoming a curse for us' (Gal 3:13).

The curse pronounced by God's moral law is no empty

form of words. It is the pronouncement of the penalty that must eventually follow every transgression of that law. Some may be inclined to argue that, since they do not believe in God, they do not recognize his right either to issue commands and prohibitions or to impose penalties. But the argument is false. The Creator's moral law is written on every human heart (Rom 2:14–16). Every time we accuse someone of having done something morally wrong, every time we excuse ourselves for some moral misdemeanour, every time we tell ourselves we ought to behave better, and promise to do so next time, we are, unintentionally maybe, witnessing to the fact that the moral law is written on our hearts and that we assent to its authority and validity. It is as though, to use a New Testament metaphor, God's moral law had been put before us written out on a document, and by our accusations of others, excuses of ourselves, and moral resolves to do better, we had personally signed our names at the bottom of the document, agreeing to its authority, demands, and penalties.

Those who do not repent will find this 'document' with their own signature on it, produced as evidence against them at the final judgment. But those who do repent are assured by God himself that he has blotted out this legal bond signed by our own hand acknowledging our guilt, this 'handwriting that was against us'; and he has nailed it to the cross of Christ. God has thus advertised before the whole universe that, by dying on the cross, Christ has borne the curse of the law for all who repent and trust him, so that they can go free (see Col 2:13–15).

The cost of redemption

The ransom paid for the redemption of mankind was nothing less than the death of Christ. In fact, he himself declared that this was the main purpose of his coming to our earth: 'For even the Son of Man came not to be served but to serve, and to give his life as a ransom for many' (Mark 10:45). 'You were redeemed', says 1 Peter 1:18–19, '. . . with the precious blood of Christ.'

To grasp the immensity of the cost of the ransom, we need to remember who Christ is:

> In whom we have redemption, the forgiveness of sins.
> He is the image of the invisible God, the firstborn of all
> creation. For by him all things were created, in heaven
> and on earth . . . all things were created through him
> and for him. And he is before all things, and in him all
> things hold together. (Col 1:14–17)

In other words, the Redeemer is none other than the Creator incarnate. Jesus is both God and man. And that is how he could act as the mediator between God and men, and give himself as a ransom for all (1 Tim 2:5–6). It was not, as some people have imagined it, that Jesus, who loved mankind, had to pay this ransom to some unkind God to persuade him not to pour out his wrath on the human race. He who paid the ransom was God. And the love which moved Christ to give his life as a ransom for men was a perfect expression of the love of the Father for men; for Christ, being himself God, was and is the perfect image and expression of the invisible God. 'In this is love,' says the

New Testament, 'not that we have loved God, but that he loved us and sent his Son to be the propitiation for our sins' (1 John 4:10).

'But in that case,' says someone, 'if Jesus did not pay the ransom to God, to whom did he pay it? For he must have paid it to somebody.' But to argue like that is to forget what we noticed earlier on, that the term 'ransom' in these contexts in the New Testament is being used as a metaphor to express the cost to God and to Christ of our redemption. The cost was not a literal money payment which some third party could receive. The cost was that of suffering and death.

Suppose a lifeboat is overcrowded and in danger of sinking, and a man voluntarily jumps overboard into the ice-cold sea, knowing it will mean his death. We might well comment that he paid a very heavy price to save the lives of the remaining passengers. But it would not make sense to ask: 'To whom did he pay this price?'

But another question arises. The Bible teaches that we are all God's creatures, and therefore his property. Why then must God pay a ransom, or anything at all, to buy back his own property? Granted we have enchained ourselves in sinful habits, and have played into Satan's hands and become his prisoners. Why could not God simply exercise his almighty power, destroy Satan, break our chains, and bring back all mankind to himself by force, without having to pay any ransom?

The answer is that the question of sin is a moral question; and you cannot settle moral questions by force. There are certain things that even almighty God cannot do. He cannot do logically impossible things like drawing a square circle. Neither can he do morally unrighteous things. He cannot lie (Titus 1:2). He cannot break his own moral law. His law is the expression of his own character. Deny it, and he would deny himself; and that he cannot do (2 Tim 2:13). It was not open to him to loose us from the chains of our guilt by a simple act of arbitrary power. The only way of doing it was first to pay the penalty which his moral law demanded. And that in love he did for us. Hence the cost; hence the suffering.[1]

Freedom for what?

We earlier observed that if you buy someone in order to subject them to slavery, the price which you pay cannot be called a ransom. Now Christ has paid the ransom to deliver people from the guilt of their sins and give them freedom. But freedom for what? Well, obviously not so that they can now carry on sinning with impunity. For sin is addictive and makes slaves of those who constantly and unrepentantly practise it (Rom 6:16–23). Here then is a statement of what Christ redeems his disciples *from* and what he redeems them *for*:

> For the grace of God has appeared, bringing salvation for all people, training us to renounce ungodliness and worldly passions, and to live self-controlled, upright, and godly lives in the present age, waiting for our blessed hope, the appearing of the glory of our great God and Saviour Jesus Christ, who gave himself for us

1 To consider again the question of Christ's payment of the penalty of sin, please see chapters 4 and 5.

to redeem us from all lawlessness and to purify for himself
a people for his own possession who are zealous for good
works. (Titus 2:11-14)

We must leave to a later chapter the question of how
Christ guarantees that this new way of life shall turn out to
be a life of freedom, not of religious slavery. For the moment,
let us notice that the New Testament makes it quite clear
that we are not given the full fruits of our redemption here
and now. Included in the benefits which Christ's ransom has
obtained for us is the 'redemption of our [physical] bodies'.
But for that we must wait until the second coming of Christ
(Rom 8:18-25; Phil 3:20-21).

On the other hand, God does here and now give to all
who repent and put their faith in Christ the gift of the Holy
Spirit. That Holy Spirit assures all believers of the reliability
of all God's promises, and is himself the earnest and pledge
of the full inheritance that will one day be theirs, when God
redeems all his promises and takes to himself in heaven the
people whom he once purchased with the blood of his Son
(Eph 1:13-14; Acts 20:28).

CHAPTER 7

Eternal Life

In the Here and Now

One of the most majestic claims that Christ ever made when he was here on earth was that he had the authority to give men and women eternal life (John 17:1–3).

That claim, as we know, has often been ridiculed. Some critics have supposed that Jesus was promising his followers that they would never die physically and then, on the basis of this supposition, they have concluded that Jesus must have been a deluded religious fanatic, since he himself died very soon thereafter and so have all his followers ever since.

But this criticism is based on sheer ignorance of what Jesus said. The merest glance at the New Testament shows that Jesus not only warned his disciples that he would shortly be crucified, but told them that after he was gone they must be prepared to lay down their lives for his sake (Luke 9:22; 12:4; John 16:1–3). Whatever else it meant, Jesus' claim that he could give his followers eternal life did not mean that they would never die physically.

Other, more serious, critics have supposed that the promised 'eternal life' is something which good people are supposed to get after they leave this world: in other words, 'they go to heaven when they die'. The critics then scorn the whole idea as a dangerous and enervating fairy story. Starving men and women, they say, dream of beef steaks; similarly the poor and the oppressed, the disappointed and the ill, invent an imaginary heaven in order to dull life's pain and to alleviate their miseries. But atheists, they claim, have no need of any such drug. They have the courage and intelligence to struggle to improve their lives, and in the end to face death's stark realities without drugging their mind with hopes of an imaginary heaven in some distant future.

Now it is perfectly true that the New Testament does teach that believers 'go to heaven when they die', though it prefers to phrase it somewhat differently: they 'depart and be with Christ', or they are 'away from the body and at home with the Lord' (Phil 1:23; 2 Cor 5:8). But the critics' charge that this hope of a future heaven necessarily weakens, if not destroys, people's struggle to make the most of their life here on earth, is patently false. The New Testament makes it abundantly clear that eternal life is not something we get when we die and go to heaven. It is a life which we can receive and enjoy here and now on earth—long before we die and go to heaven. It is, so to speak, another dimension to life, above and beyond the mere physical, emotional, aesthetic, and intellectual life which human beings naturally enjoy. It is the life to which Christ pointed when he said, 'Man shall not live by bread alone, but by every word which proceeds from the mouth of God' (Matt 4:4).

Imagine, if you can, a marriage that consisted of nothing more than physical union, a marriage in which the man and the woman never spoke to each other, never shared their innermost thoughts, their hopes, their joys, their fears and sorrows, their love of music or art, and never got to know each other. Such a marriage would be little more than the mating of animals. It would lack the truly human dimension. Similarly, a human being who is content to enjoy life at the physical, emotional, aesthetic, and intellectual levels, but knows nothing of spiritual fellowship with God is missing the highest level of life in the here and now. Moreover, he is in the gravest danger of missing eternal life in the world to come as well. The New Testament is explicit: 'Whoever believes in the Son', it says, 'has eternal life'. Note the present tense of the verb: has it here and now. On the other hand, it adds the warning: 'whoever does not obey the Son shall not see life, but the wrath of God remains on him' (John 3:36).

Here, then, we need to grasp another distinction: the eternal life which the New Testament speaks of is not the same thing as eternal existence. All human beings survive the death of their bodies; all will exist eternally. But some will exist in such a spiritual state that the Bible calls it, not 'eternal life,' but 'the second death' (Rev 20:11–15; we shall study this topic towards the end of this book).

At this point some critics will, perhaps, protest that all talk of an eternal life which can be enjoyed in this life is a form of psychological self-deception. It is mere subjectivism; it answers to no objective reality. But the same thing could be said about art appreciation; and it would be equally fallacious. True, there are people who can look at a masterpiece of art and see little more in it than blobs of paint on a canvas; and blind people can have little concept of the world of visual art at all. But that does not prove that the world of art does not exist, or that the enjoyment of art is psychological self-deception. Some physically blind people, of course, do not wish for sight. I once knew a man who had possessed a little sight as a child, but soon lost it and became totally blind. He often told me that he would not want sight even if he were offered it. He was content as he was. He was afraid that if he received sight, he would become confused with the thousands of things he could see, and life would become very complicated. He preferred the simplicity of life without sight.

Similarly, there are many who feel that life would become too complicated, and would involve them in too many radical changes, if they admitted the existence of God and the possibility of receiving eternal life. They prefer the simplicity of atheism. And so they claim that 'God' and 'eternal' life are imaginary entities. But their claiming it does not prove that it is so; it shows rather that they are spiritually blind.

What, then, does it mean to have eternal life?

1. *To have eternal life means to share the life of God.* In New Testament terminology, until people enter into a personal relationship with God and come to know him, they are dead. Not physically dead, but spiritually.

The famous parable of the Prodigal Son furnishes a good example of the use of the word 'dead' in this sense. Talking to the elder brother after the return of the prodigal, the father says: 'It was fitting to celebrate and be glad, for this your brother was dead, and is alive; he was lost, and is found' (Luke 15:32).

The prodigal had turned his back on his father, abandoned home, gone into a far country. He had no love of, or interest in, his father. He never communicated with him; he had no wish to share his father's interests or life. As far as his father was concerned, he was dead.

The prodigal 'came to life' when he repented, returned home and was reconciled with his father. Similarly, when people who have ignored God and have been spiritually dead, repent and are reconciled with God, they begin to live spiritually.

But there is more to it than that. When people repent and turn to God, they do not only discover God, like someone might discover the glorious world of art to which he had previously been completely dead. When people repent, turn to God, and put their faith in Christ, God generates within them a new life that was never there before. To use New Testament terminology once more, God makes them alive. He begets in them his own spiritual life, just as a human father transmits his own physical life to the child he begets.

> But God, being rich in mercy, because of the great love
> with which he loved us, even when we were dead in
> our trespasses, made us alive together with Christ—by
> grace you have been saved. (Eph 2:4–5)

An analogy. An electric light bulb, enclosed in its protective wrapping does not yet shine. Take it out of its wrapping, put it into the socket on a lampstand, and place it in a room that is already brilliantly lit by a large central electric light. The bulb is now surrounded by light from the central light source; but it still does not shine itself; it is still 'dead'. And it will remain 'dead' until it is connected to the same electric current as that which empowers the central light. But when that happens, and the electric current surges through the bulb—watch how the bulb comes 'alive'.

2. *The gift of eternal life establishes a personal relationship between its recipient and God.* A computer can learn to recognize the voice of the man who uses it. All the man needs to do is to speak in the presence of the computer and the computer will reproduce all he says in written form on paper. But the computer will never know the man in the same way as the man's child or wife knows him; it will never love the man as his sons and daughters do. The computer does not have human life. But when the man begat his children and transmitted to them his own life, along with that life the children received the ability to know and love their father and to enjoy an ever deepening relationship with him. Similarly, when God transmits his own spiritual life to people, quickens and regenerates them, it forms a relationship between him and them; and they know him and love him. That is why the New Testament says that 'eternal life is to know God and Jesus Christ' (John 17:3), and to share the very life of God through Christ (1 John 1:1–4).

3. *Eternal life: a present gift, an everlasting possession.* And that explains how eternal life can be, as its name declares, eternal. When God forms this spiritual relationship with a person and shares his own life with that person, that

relationship is by definition eternal. The physical death of the body does not end it, and cannot destroy it. Once God has formed a personal relationship with someone through the gift of eternal life, he will remain loyal to that person and maintain the relationship forever. 'I give them [my sheep] eternal life,' said Christ, 'and they will never perish' (John 10:28). 'For God so loved the world, that he gave his only Son, that whoever believes on him should not perish but have eternal life' (John 3:16).

Eternal life, then, is unaffected by the death of the body. The human body, as we know it here on earth, is likened by the New Testament to a tent, well suited to our temporary, earthly pilgrimage, but comparatively fragile, easily collapsible and taken down. By contrast, at the resurrection each believer will receive a glorified body, designed to express his redeemed and perfected personality, and described by the New Testament as 'a building from God, a house . . . eternal in the heavens' (2 Cor 5:1).

Moreover, along with eternal life come all those other eternal things which God gives to all who are willing to receive Christ. So the New Testament points out that salvation is eternal (Heb 5:9); redemption and its effects are eternal (Heb 9:12); the inheritance promised to those that trust God is eternal (Heb 9:15); and the glory which life's experiences and sufferings will effect for those who love God is likewise eternal (2 Cor 4:17). And the wonderful thing about it is that eternal life is a free gift, which is given to all those who, in true repentance and faith, accept Jesus Christ as both Saviour and Lord: 'For the wages of sin is death, but the free gift of God is eternal life in Christ Jesus our Lord' (Rom 6:23).

Eternal life's potential

Eternal life, like physical life, is not a static thing. A baby, as soon as it is born, has physical life; but in the weeks, months, and years ahead it has to learn to develop its potential. So it is with eternal life: it is full of potential, and therefore always full of hope for the future. Those who have received eternal life are exhorted in the New Testament to 'lay hold on' the eternal life to which God has called them, just as a young man who has the potential to become a world class athlete might be encouraged not to neglect his gift, but to exploit it to the full (1 Tim 4:7-8; 6:11-12). And the chief reward for developing the potential of eternal life, is the ever-increasing ability to enjoy that life. 'The one who sows to the Spirit,' says the New Testament, 'will from the Spirit reap eternal life' (Gal 6:8). The more an athlete runs, the more he develops his heart, lungs, muscles, and breathing; and the more he develops them, the more he enjoys his running.

Of course, serious training will demand of the athlete, discipline, self-denial, singleness of purpose, and hard work. And if the athlete hopes to win a prize in the championship games, he will have to keep the rules of the game. If he does not keep those rules, he will not lose his life, but he will certainly not win any prize. And so it is with eternal life. To develop its potential and reap the maximum rewards, those who possess it must be prepared to 'lay aside every weight, and sin which clings so closely, and let [them] run with endurance the race set before [them]' (Heb 12:1). They must be ready to deny themselves, to take up their cross daily and follow Christ.

And they must learn to develop self-control and 'to keep the rules of the game'. Otherwise, they will be disqualified and get no prize (1 Cor 9:24–27; 2 Tim 2:5).

But the wonderful thing about eternal life is this: it enables those who possess it to live in such a way that the experiences, duties, pleasures, and pains of this passing world can be given eternal significance and be made to yield an eternal reward (John 12:25; 2 Pet 1:5–11).

The possibility of knowing that we have eternal life: Some people, even some religious people, maintain that it is impossible to be sure in this life that we have eternal life. It is good, therefore, to have the plain statement of the New Testament on the topic. We shall consider it in depth in a later chapter; but here, to begin with, is the statement itself:

> And this is the testimony, that God gave us eternal life, and this life is in his Son. Whoever has the Son has life; whoever does not have the Son of God does not have life. I write these things to you who believe in the name of the Son of God that you may know that you have eternal life. (1 John 5:11–13)

CHAPTER 8

Repentance

More than Being Sorry

Up to this point, we have studied the terms which the New Testament uses to describe what God has done to reconcile, justify, ransom, redeem, and regenerate mankind. Now we must begin to study the terms that describe what we must do to benefit from what God has done, is doing, and will yet do.

The first of these terms is *repentance*. The very first public announcement by Christ was this: 'The time is fulfilled, and the kingdom of God is at hand; repent and believe in the gospel' (Mark 1:15).

According to Christ, repentance is an occasion of great joy: 'I tell you, there is joy before the angels of God over one sinner who repents' (Luke 15:10). Repentance is also a healthy thing. Like rain which softens the earth and allows seeds to germinate and grow, so repentance opens the way to spiritual life: 'To the Gentiles also God has granted repentance that leads to life', is how the New Testament describes it (Acts 11:18).

Repentance, however, is a complex thing and to be true, healthy, and effective, it needs to have all its necessary ingredients. Full repentance, for instance, may well involve healthy sorrow: 'For godly sorrow produces a repentance that leads to salvation without regret' (2 Cor 7:10). On the other hand, sorrow that falls short of full repentance is not only ineffective in that it does not lead to salvation and life: it is also morbid and destructive. 'Worldly grief produces death' (2 Cor 7:10).

A vivid example of this is Judas, who betrayed Christ. When he saw that Jesus was condemned, he 'repented himself,' that is, he 'changed his mind'. He tried to undo the evil thing he had done, but that proved impossible. He could, of course, have run to the cross and cried to Jesus for mercy and forgiveness as the dying thief did. But no! His kind of repentance was not the full and healthy repentance to which the New Testament calls us. It was simply regret and remorse. It did not lead to life and salvation. Quite the reverse—Judas went away and hanged himself (Matt 27:3-5).

In the course of translation and common usage, the New Testament meaning of repentance has often become distorted and so we shall have to examine it very carefully. In the original Greek of the New Testament two words are used for repentance:

1. *metanoia* and its related verb *metanoeo*. The basic meaning of these words is 'a change of mind'. Various emotions and feelings may, or may not, lead to, accompany, or spring from, this change of mind. But its primary element is intellectual. It is an exercise of the moral judgment.

2. *metamelomai* and the impersonal verb, *metamelei*. These two verbs also are used to express the idea of repentance; but they carry more emphasis on sorrow for having done something.

Repentance, then, is primarily a change of mind, a reversal of one's previous moral judgment, a repudiation of one's previous behaviour. It has in it a negative element. So the New Testament speaks of repentance from false and evil things, e.g. 'repentance from dead works' (Heb 6:1). But it also has a positive element: 'repentance towards God' (Acts 20:21). Notice how the following passage emphasizes the intellectual element in repentance (our thoughts and God's thoughts), the negative element (forsaking one's evil way) and the positive element (returning to the Lord).

> Let the wicked forsake his way, and the unrighteous man his thoughts; and let him return unto the Lord, and he will have mercy upon him; and to our God, for he will abundantly pardon. For my thoughts are not your thoughts, neither are your ways my ways, declares the Lord. (Isa 55:7-8 RV)

Repentance in three areas

There are three major areas in which we are called upon to repent:

1. *In relation to God:* Obviously, if we are atheists, repentance will mean abandoning our atheism and acknowledging the existence of God. But it is not only atheists who need repentance towards God. It is possible to believe in the

existence of God, and yet in practice to ignore him, to disregard all his commands to repent and be saved, to flout his laws and to live as if he did not exist. To a greater or lesser degree, this has been true of us all. 'All we like sheep have gone astray; we have turned—everyone—to his own way' (Isa 53:6). Repentance means nothing less than this: turning to God from idols (anything we hold in place of the one true God) to serve the living and true God (1 Thess 1:9).

2. *In relation to ourselves:* The New Testament requires two distinct levels of repentance. Since this is easily overlooked, we begin with an illustration of the difference between the two.

A man of fifty is very unwell. He goes to a doctor. After a thorough examination, the doctor tells him that the cause of his illness is excessive smoking. 'Yes, I realize that now,' says the man, 'and I repent of it. Please give me something to help me give it up.'

So far so good. The man has repented of the individual sin of smoking. But the doctor says, 'Well, you are wise to give up smoking; but giving up smoking cannot save you. Your lungs are virtually destroyed, and your heart is severely damaged. The only thing that can save you is to allow a surgeon to perform a heart-lung transplant operation on you.'

Now the crucial question is: will the man be willing to repent at this more basic level? That is, will he agree with the doctor that his condition is so bad that merely giving up smoking cannot save him: only a new heart and new lungs can save him?

Suppose the man rejects the doctor's verdict: 'No, I am not prepared to have this drastic operation. I am not as ill as you say. I am confident that if I give up smoking, I shall be all right.' What will happen? He will very shortly die!

On the other hand, if he repents at this basic level, agrees with the doctor's diagnosis, submits to the operation, and so receives the heart and lungs of another person, it will still be important that he repents of the sin of smoking. Indeed the surgeon may well say to him as he leaves hospital: 'I insist that you now give up smoking entirely. And if ever you succumb to the temptation to smoke again, come at once and I can give you something to help you overcome the temptation.'

So it is with us. God's verdict is that we are so bad that repenting of individual sins, important as that is, cannot save us. We need what we might call radical repentance. This means agreeing with God's verdict not only regarding our sins, but also ourselves. It is a question not only of what we have done, but of what we are. God's verdict is not only that we have sinned in the past and that in the present we still come short of his standards of holiness (Rom 3:23), but that by our very nature we are 'children of wrath' (Eph 2:1–3). Our very nature is sinful and calls forth God's displeasure. This does not mean, of course, that every part of us is as bad as bad could be. It does mean that no part of us is free from the damage that sin has caused.

A tree does not become an apple tree by bearing apples. It bears apples because it is already by nature an apple tree. Take every visible apple off the tree and it is still an apple tree! Simply confessing our individual sins, few or many, is like cutting the apples off the tree. It does not face, or deal with, the problem of what we are by nature in ourselves. The fact is that we are, as John the Baptist put it, 'bad trees' that deserve to be cut down and thrown into the fire (Matt 3:10).

At this point, however, many people refuse to accept God's verdict. They refuse to repent. They are prepared to admit that they have done wrong things, outrageously wrong things, perhaps. They may even admit that there are dark areas in their character. But they cling to the idea that all they need to do is to repent of their past wrong deeds, and seek God's help to break their bad habits. That, they hope, will leave them the basically good people that they always felt they were, with a good chance of qualifying for God's heaven.

But this is an illusion, as Christ himself pointed out: 'For no good tree bears bad fruit, nor again does a bad tree bear good fruit, for each tree is known by its own fruit. For figs are not gathered from thorn bushes, nor are grapes picked from a bramble bush' (Luke 6:43–44). It is no use for a thorn bush to say: 'I admit I have produced quite a few thorns. But I am not a thorn bush really: basically I am a fig tree.'

Radical repentance, then, means giving up our own estimate of ourselves and agreeing with God's verdict that repenting from individual sins cannot save us. We need new spiritual life from a source outside of ourselves. That source is Christ, who died for us, and now lives to be our Saviour.

This is, in fact, the historical significance of Christian baptism. Baptism, so the New Testament explains (Rom 6:3-4), is a symbolic burial, by which the candidate publicly confesses that he has accepted God's verdict that he was worthy of nothing else but to be executed and buried. It is not a magical operation by which the bad parts of a person's character are somehow washed away, leaving the good parts to grow and flourish. In baptism the whole person is buried, just as in the physical world when a man is executed for murder, the whole man is put to death and buried: not just his bad temper or jealousy which made him commit the murder. Similarly, when a person is executed for murder, that death puts an end to his whole life. It does not just cancel his past life up to the present, leaving him to live the rest of his life the best he can. No, it is final. The whole life is finished. The death never needs to be (nor can be) repeated.

So when Christ died for our sins, he died once, and he will never die again, for he will never need to (see Rom 6:8-11). His one death paid the complete penalty for the sins of those who accept him as Saviour, for the sins of their whole life—past, present and future. When someone is baptized, therefore, he is also simultaneously declaring that he has accepted Christ as the substitute and Saviour provided for him by God; and that in accepting Christ he has become one with him, as a man and woman become one when they marry (1 Cor 6:15-17). Therefore, in God's sight, when Christ died, the believer died, when Christ was buried, he was buried; legally that was the end of his sinful self forever. He is saying what the Apostle Paul said: 'I have been crucified with Christ' (Gal 2:19-21).

Baptism, thus, is also a symbolic resurrection. It signifies that just as God raised Christ from the dead, so God gives to everyone who accepts Christ an altogether new spiritual life; not the old life now somewhat improved, but a new life which he never had before. It is nothing other than the life of Christ himself. The believer can therefore truly say (to complete the Apostle Paul's statement):

> I have been crucified with Christ. It is no longer I who live, but Christ who lives in me. And the life I now live in the flesh I live by faith in the Son of God, who loved me and gave himself for me. (Gal 2:20)

It goes without saying, of course, that baptism is only a symbol. It does not effect the death and resurrection which it symbolizes. It is like a wedding ring. An unmarried woman could put on a wedding ring, but that would not mean that she was now married. The ring only becomes significant after she has agreed to accept a man as her husband. So one has to repent in the radical sense we have been discussing and personally accept Christ as Saviour before being baptized. Otherwise baptism is an empty symbol, a representation of something that is not true.

3. The next area in which we are called upon to repent is *in relation to our sins*. The person who has radically repented, and has received Christ is now legally free. He no longer needs to struggle to improve himself in order to gain acceptance with God: he already is accepted. But precisely because God has for Christ's sake accepted him, he will be expected to develop a truly Christian way of life. That will mean reading God's Word to discover what attitudes and acts God regards as sinful, and then repenting of them, and seeking Christ's power and strength to eliminate them. And when he falls to weakness and temptation, as he will from time to time, he is required to confess it to God. The promise is: 'If we confess our sins, he is faithful

and just to forgive us our sins, and to cleanse us from all unrighteousness' (1 John 1:9). This kind of repentance, then, is a life-time's occupation. It will need to be repeated daily (Rev 2:5, 16, 21; 3:3).

Further features of true repentance

1. Repentance is not simply a matter of words. It will issue in behaviour that demonstrates the repentance to be genuine. 'Bear fruit in keeping with repentance', said John the Baptist (Matt 3:8).

2. At the same time, repentance does not merit or earn salvation. Forgiveness of sin is not dependent on the strength of our sorrow for sin, nor can it be earned by any works of penance. Forgiveness remains an utterly free and unearned gift given to bankrupt sinners and accepted solely through faith. That is why 'repentance towards God' needs to be accompanied by 'faith in our Lord Jesus Christ' (Acts 20:21).

3. Repentance is urgent. 'God . . . now . . . commands all people everywhere to repent' (Acts 17:30). Christ himself reminded us: 'Unless you repent, you will all likewise perish' (Luke 13:3, 5).

CHAPTER 9

Faith

Not a Leap in the Dark

In our last chapter, we saw that in order to benefit from all that God has done, is doing, and will yet do for mankind, our first step must be *repentance* towards God. But there is a second, and that is *faith* in our Lord Jesus Christ (Acts 20:21).

According to the New Testament, the conditions of salvation are: (*a*) 'If you confess with your mouth that Jesus is Lord' (that is objectively as the Son of God, and subjectively as your personal Lord), and (*b*) if you will 'believe in your heart that God raised him from the dead, you will be saved' (Rom 10:9). The question that immediately arises is this: how does such faith come?

Difficulties with faith: faith and science

Nowadays many people can be heard to remark: 'We would like to believe in God and Christ, but it is very difficult for us to believe. To us faith seems such an arbitrary thing. In science you can have evidence and proof, and you don't need faith. But with Christianity you just have to make up your mind to believe without any evidence and without any proof. It is like jumping out of a window on a pitch black night with your eyes shut, hoping that you will land safely somewhere.'

Others feel that faith is like artistic ability: you either have it or you don't have it, and there is nothing you can do about it.

Neither of these views is true. Moreover the idea that science does not involve faith is also false. In fact, faith is fundamental to the scientific endeavour. Albert Einstein said: 'Science can only be created by those who are thoroughly imbued with the aspiration toward truth and understanding. This source of feeling, however, springs from the sphere of religion. To this there also belongs the faith in the possibility that the regulations valid for the world of existence are rational, that is, comprehensible to reason. I cannot conceive of a genuine scientist without that profound faith. The situation may be expressed by an image: science without religion is lame, religion without science is blind.'[1]

---

1 *Science and Religion* (1941); *Science, Philosophy and Religion, A Symposium*, New York: The Conference on Science, Philosophy and Religion in Their Relation to the Democratic Way of Life, Inc., 1941; later published in *Out of My Later Years* (1950).

There have, of course, been both scientists and philosophers who have questioned whether the universe which the scientists profess to describe is actually there. They have suggested that it only exists in the minds and formulae of the scientists themselves. The scientists' theories, they claim, answer to no objective reality. But this is, understandably, the view of a tiny minority.

The great majority believes that the universe which they investigate, either directly or through their instruments, is actually there. They do not create it by their observations, measurements, hypotheses, theories, experiments, and interpretations. They accept its existence as a given. True, they have discovered details in it, like elementary particles, which they did not previously know existed. But these details existed before they discovered them. The scientist, then, does not create the universe by his studies—he simply tries to understand it. And for that purpose he submits his mind to the evidence presented by the universe; and he judges the truth of his theories by the extent to which they can be shown, by experiment, to explain the evidence.

Now the Bible asserts that the universe is there because God put it there. He created it. He spoke it into existence by his creative Word (Gen 1; John 1:1-4; Heb 11:3). It is a revelation of God's mind, an expression of his creatorial thinking. In studying this revelation, a scientist, whether he knows it or not, is thinking God's thoughts after him, as Kepler said.[2]

2 For more on Johannes Kepler's conclusions about God and scientific investigation, see his *Harmonices Mundi* (*The Harmony of the World*). Trans. E. J. Aiton, A. M.Duncan and J. V. Field. American Philosophical Society, 1997.

Similarly the Bible asserts that the same God who has revealed himself through creation has likewise revealed himself to us through his Son Jesus Christ. Christ is not the creation of the church or the product of religious and theological speculation. He is called in the Bible the Word of God because in him God has revealed himself and spoken to us men and women far more directly and far more fully than ever he could through creation. In creation, God has told us of his power and majesty. In Christ, the Word of God, he has told out his heart. Our task, then, is to study the evidence provided by God's self-revelation in Christ, just as the scientist studies the evidence provided by God's self-revelation in creation.

Now it is the fact that scientists are wary of scientific explanations that are too facile. They have learned by experience that the universe is constantly presenting us with the unexpected, and with phenomena that can only be explained in terms that seem to defy ordinary common sense. But they do not on that account reject these difficult explanations out of hand. Indeed, they are prepared to trust them rather than common sense; and the ultimate vindication of their trust is that when they design experiments on their basis, they work.

It is so with God's self-revelation to man through Jesus Christ. As we know, the New Testament claims that Christ is both God and man. This assertion seems to many people to be at complete variance with common sense and when they find that not even the Bible itself offers a complete explanation of how he can be both God and man simultaneously, they are inclined to dismiss it as a primitive myth. But this is hardly a scientific reaction, as we have now seen.

Those who encountered Jesus Christ when he was here on earth discovered in the first place, of course, that he was genuinely human. At the same time, they found that he exhibited indisputable phenomena which demonstrated that he was much more than human. Christ's explanation was that he was both man and God at the same time. And if we ask how we can be expected to believe this explanation, the New Testament will point us to investigations and experiments that we can make that will prove to us that this explanation is true (John 7:16–17; 20:30–31). Indeed, the New Testament claims that not only was Jesus Christ a real historical figure: risen from the dead, he is a living person with whom we can come in contact.

Why read the New Testament?

But at this someone may well object: 'It is no use my reading the New Testament. For the New Testament to do me any good, I would first have to believe, even before I read it, that what it says is true. And since I don't believe it is true, there is no point in my reading it.' But this objection rests on a misunderstanding, for one does not have to believe that the New Testament is true before reading it. On the other hand, if you have never read the New Testament seriously, you cannot honestly and scientifically know in advance that it is not true. You would not take that attitude towards, say, newspapers. From having read many newspapers, you know that newspapers are liable to contain things that are not true.

But you do not for that reason refuse to read newspapers. You read the newspapers, confident that you can distinguish truth from falsehood; and if you cannot for the moment do so, you suspend your judgment. Read the New Testament in the same way; and then, when you have read it, and only then, make up your mind as to whether Jesus spoke the truth or not. Faith in Jesus could not possibly come unless you first listen to what he says; to refuse even to listen to him, is not a sign of intellectual prowess: it is obscurantism.

Of course the issues at stake are much greater than when reading a report in a newspaper. Indeed, as we saw at the start, the first condition for salvation, as laid down by the New Testament, is confession of Jesus as Lord! This involves, of course, accepting Jesus as one's personal Lord and Master, and being prepared to confess him as such before the world. But it involves more than that. In the Old Testament God says, 'I, I am the Lord, and besides me there is no saviour' (Isa 43:11). 'The Lord' is a synonym for God the Creator. If Jesus were not this Lord, if he were not God in human form, then he could save nobody. The claim is stupendous and the New Testament will certainly not ask us to believe it without supplying us with evidence on which to base that faith. So the question is, therefore, what evidence is there to lead us to believe that Jesus is Lord in this sense?

The evidence of Christ's own statements

It may at first sound naive, but the main reason for believing that Jesus is the Son of God is that he himself said he was. It raises at once the question of his veracity. And very properly so; for even when all the evidence has been stated that points unmistakably to his deity, the ultimate question that the human soul has to decide when confronted with Jesus Christ is: Is he true? Does he speak the truth? What value can we put on his often repeated 'Truly, truly, I say to you.' The situation is the same with God. The ultimate question is not 'Is there a God?' but 'Is God true? Is he to be trusted?' The Apostle James remarks somewhat wryly that the demons believe that there is one God (Jas 2:19). But they neither trust nor obey him. Many people who likewise believe that God exists, do not trust him, nor are they prepared to stake their lives here or in the world to come on the truthfulness of his word. They feel they can't.

'But you cannot expect us to believe', says someone, 'that Jesus is the Son of God, simply because he said so himself. It is not reasonable.' Christ's contemporaries raised the same question: 'You bear witness of yourself,' they said; and from that they drew the conclusion: 'your witness is not true', that is, it is not valid (John 8:13).

Christ immediately challenged that unwarranted conclusion: 'Even if I do bear witness about myself,' he said, 'my testimony is true, for I know where I came from and where I am going, but you do not know where I come from or where I am going' (John 8:14). He was, of course, referring to heaven as the place from which he came and to which he was soon to return. He spoke with the authority of personal experience. It was altogether unwarrantable to conclude that, because he was the only one who could tell them of these things, his testimony was necessarily not valid.

Let's use an analogy. The people who lived in the Mediterranean basin three thousand years ago held that if you stood facing the noon-day sun, it was an unchallengeable fact that the sun had earlier risen on your left and would later go down on your right. Now suppose one day there arrived a lone man from South Africa, the first ever from that country to visit the Mediterranean basin. He could have said that in the country he came from, if you stood facing the noonday sun, it was an unchallengeable fact that the sun had earlier risen on your right and would later go down on your left. The question is: would the local Mediterranean people have been right to believe him? What he said was the opposite of all they had ever experienced, and went against their contemporary science and cosmology. They might well have said: 'You are the only one ever to have told us this. We cannot believe it just because you say so. Your testimony is not valid. We cannot believe that there is any such country where the sun behaves as you say it does.'

He then might have replied: 'Even if I am the only one to tell you this, yet my testimony is valid. I know the country from which I come and to which I shall soon return. You do not know that country.' And he would have been right. His testimony was valid, and if they had believed it, they would have been believing what was in fact true.

Of course, it may well have been difficult for the Mediterranean people to believe the stranger from South Africa; for there were many so-called 'travellers' tales' which told about people who claimed to have been to the ends of the earth and to have seen there fantastically marvellous things. None of it was true. It was all pure imagination. How could they then distinguish between these travellers' tales and what the South African said? And how can we distinguish between superstitious religious legends and what Christ said?

Christ himself replied to such questions by pointing out that though his own bare statements were valid by themselves, there was additional evidence that corroborated his claims: and that was his miracles (John 5:36). He did, so he claimed, works of such kind and significance as no one else had ever done (John 15:24). To these we must turn in our next chapter.

CHAPTER 10

Faith

A Response to Evidence

We concluded the preceding chapter by saying that Christ's statements are corroborated by the miracles he did. Now the New Testament calls his miracles *signs* because they point to the truth of his claim to be the Son of God:

> Now Jesus did many other signs in the presence of the disciples, which are not written in this book; but these are written so that you may believe that Jesus is the Christ, the Son of God, and that by believing you may have life in his name. (John 20:30-31)

The evidence of Christ's miracles

All right, says someone, but what evidence have we that the miracles recorded in the Gospels actually happened?

We were not there to see them happen. How can we be sure that these records are true? And what was the point of these miracles anyway? Does not the Bible claim that other people too, like Elijah, did miracles? But that did not prove that any of them was the Son of God. How then do Jesus' miracles prove that he is?

For the historical evidence that Jesus actually performed miracles we are dependent on the testimony of the Christian apostles. We have no compelling a priori reason not to trust them, for the idea that miracles are impossible has not been proven by science; it is an unproved and unprovable axiom of certain (but not all) worldviews.

The question, then, is not a scientific one, but a historical one: is the testimony of the apostles reliable?

We may be sure, in the first place, that the apostles were not knowing and deliberate liars. The apostle John lays it down as axiomatic that 'no lie is of the truth' (1 John 2:21). Lies, in his estimation, were unacceptable, even in the cause of propagating the greater truth, and altogether incompatible with him who claimed to be the truth (John 14:6), and who strictly forbade all false witness (Matt 5:33–37). When, therefore, John tells us that he and his fellow apostles saw Jesus do miracles in front of their very eyes, it is clear that he believes that he is recording actual historical events.

Secondly, we should notice John's claim that, when he records Jesus' miracles, he is not simply repeating hearsay. He and his fellow-apostles were first-hand witnesses. The miracles which they report were done 'in the presence of his disciples' (John 12:37).

But thirdly, and most importantly, we should notice the nature of Christ's miracles. They were not only historical events. They present us with another kind of evidence that challenges us even today with an immediacy that transcends history. The Greek of the New Testament alerts us to this. Christ's miracles, it says, were not only works of special power (Greek: *dynamis*), and not only astonishing wonders (Greek: *teras*) that arrested people's attention: they were also signs (Greek: *semeion*) that pointed beyond themselves to something far more important than the physical miracle itself.

Take, for example, the miracle of the feeding of the five thousand (John 6). At its first level of significance, it was performed by Christ out of his compassion for the people's physical hunger. But that was not its only, and not even its main, purpose. The people naturally got hungry the next day as well. But the record itself tells us that when they came to Jesus clamouring for a repeat of this physical miracle, he refused to repeat it. Why? If he did have these miraculous powers, why did he not go on using them day after day until physical hunger was banished from the earth? And why does he not still do it today? Because, so he said, they had failed to see, or else were deliberately ignoring, the higher purpose, the significance of this miraculous sign (John 6:26). The miracle was meant to alert them not only to the fact that Jesus was their Creator in human form, but that he had come down from heaven to offer himself to them as the Bread of Life to satisfy their spiritual hunger. The stomach, being itself material, can be satisfied with material things. But the human spirit, deriving as it does from God who is spirit, can never be fully satisfied with material things nor with merely aesthetic or intellectual pleasures. It needs fellowship with a person, and that person none other than its Creator. Without him, the human spirit is doomed to perpetual hunger, which ten thousand physical miracles would never quench.

At this level we can test the truth of this miracle story ourselves. It offers us a diagnosis of human need. It says we are spiritually hungry, whether or not we consciously know what (or rather, whom) we are hungry for. Is this true? We know our own hearts; we can decide, each one for himself, whether this diagnosis is true.

Multitudes, of course, have been taught and trained to suppress their spiritual hunger. Some have succeeded and will honestly claim that they feel no pangs of spiritual hunger. But that can be an alarming symptom. We are told that when people are physically starving without any food whatever, it is at first very painful. But after a while the pain goes away and does not return until death is imminent and inevitable. It can be similarly so with spiritual starvation and its final stage, the second death.

But to those who recognize their spiritual hunger, Christ offers himself as the Living Bread. Do they long for that spiritual dimension of life that is eternal fellowship with God, that begins here on earth and extends beyond the grave into God's heaven? Christ guarantees that he can give that (John 6:28–58). Do they long to have their spirit freed from the shadow cast on it by the guilt and bondage of sin? Christ through his death can give them that as well (John 8:31–36).

How then can we know that he is true, that he is, as he claims to be, our Creator in human form? In the same way as we know a loaf of bread can genuinely satisfy our physical hunger. By coming to it, trusting it, taking it, eating it. So to those who recognize the truth of his diagnosis of their spiritual hunger, Christ says: 'I am the bread of life. He who comes to me shall not hunger, and whoever believes on me shall never thirst' (John 6:35). They who come and believe discover that he is true.

But now we turn to another kind of evidence somewhat different from that supplied by Christ's miracles.

The evidence supplied by Christ's death

According to the New Testament, it is not only, it is not even chiefly, Christ's miracles that are intended by God to provoke our faith in him. It is rather Christ's death on the cross:

> For Jews demand signs [that is, miracles] and Greeks seek wisdom, but we preach Christ crucified ... For I decided to know nothing among you except Jesus Christ and him crucified. ... that your faith might not rest in the wisdom of men but in the power of God. ... For the word of the cross is folly to those who are perishing, but to us who are being saved it is the power of God. (1 Cor 1:22-23; 2:2, 5; 1:18)

How, then, does the cross of Christ provoke our faith, that he is our Creator incarnate, the Son of the living God? It does so because *the cross of God's Son reveals what God is really like.*

Obviously, if ever our hearts are going to believe in, to love, and to trust, God, we need first to know what God's heart is like. Now philosophy cannot tell us that. It can speculate about God, but it cannot tell us what is in his heart. (It cannot even tell us what is going on in the heart of the man next door.) Nor can God's creation tell us. It can let us see his power; but it cannot unequivocally show us his heart. If ever we were going to know what God's heart's attitude towards us is like, then God had to take the initiative and reveal himself, and do so in terms which we human beings could understand. Hence the incarnation, the Word of God made flesh.

But just here God, so to speak, had a problem; and it was a problem which Christ pointed out to his contemporaries. They, somewhat cynically, suggested that, to gain the public's faith and support, he ought to seek out maximum publicity and stage a whole succession of spectacular miracles. But they had not reckoned with the fundamental difficulty. 'The world cannot hate you,' he said, 'but it hates me because I testify about it that its works are evil' (John 7:1–7). His testimony sprang neither from self-righteous pride, nor from narrow-minded religious misanthropy. He was the perfect expression of God, God's own self-communication in human terms. Inevitably, therefore, he revealed the holiness of God to an unprecedented extent; and the more he did that, the more it exposed men's sinfulness, the more people resented it, and the more they resisted his claim to be the Son of God.

Understandably so. If a friend of yours says that something you have done was a mean, despicable act, you may well resent it at first; but after a while, you may console yourself with the thought that that was only his opinion, and who is he after all? You therefore decide to ignore it and to continue your friendship with him. But if someone tells you that you are a sinner worthy of God's judgment, and then adds, 'And I who tell you this am the Son of God', your natural reaction would very likely be first to ridicule his claim to be the Son of God, and then, if he insisted on it, to resist it with might and main. For if he is right, you stand condemned.

The ancient Latin poet, Lucretius, who in a long, and often majestic, work expounded the early Greek atomic theory and the then current theory of evolution for the benefit of his fellow Romans, confesses in the Introduction why these theories appealed so powerfully to him.[1] In the first place they seemed to him to prove that death ends everything: there is no afterlife; and this, in turn, relieved him of all prospect and fear of punishment for his sins in the life to come. He therefore preached these theories with all the fervour of an evangelist.

It is so with many people still. Admit Christ's claim to be the Son of God, and it immediately carries with it, they feel, the fear of a holy God, of a final judgment, and of punishment for sin. They, therefore, resist the claim and determine not to be convinced. That being so, for Christ to perform a whole succession of miracles that were purely and simply exhibitions of supernatural power, would tend to increase people's fear, strengthen their resistance, and drive them to look for alternative explanations of Christ's power. Hence, therefore, God's reliance, not chiefly on Christ's miracles to win the human heart, but on his cross. Christ himself soothed the hostility of his opponents who were enraged by his exposure of their sinfulness: 'When you have lifted

1 *De Rerum Natura*, Book I.

up [that is, crucified] the Son of Man,' he said, 'then you will know that I AM [your God, Creator and Lord] and that I do nothing on my own authority, but speak just as the Father taught me' (John 8:28).

Through the cross of his Son, God does, of course, expose our sin. And not only expose it, but exhibit it before the eyes of the whole universe. Such is the estrangement and rebellion of the human heart that, given the opportunity by God's incarnation, mankind would crucify, indeed has crucified, its Maker. Through the cross of his Son, God also demonstrates his unyielding holiness. Sin can do nothing else but incur his uncompromising displeasure. It must be punished.

But simultaneously, and above everything else, through the death of his Son, God tells out his whole heart towards his creatures. Though they have been deceived by Satan, and sin has made them his enemies, he remains loyal to them. He loves them with a love such as only a creator could have for his creatures. He does not will that any one of them should perish, but rather that all should come to repentance (2 Pet 3:9). Rather than that they should perish under the penalty for sin, he would pay that penalty at the cost of the sufferings of his divine Son himself; and so be justly free to offer to all complete and eternal redemption.

The cross proclaims that God longs for all men to be saved and come to the knowledge of the truth, that is, to discover what God is really like and how his heart stands and feels towards them. To show the world what the Father's heart is like, the Son has given himself a ransom for all, to make it possible for the longings of God's love to be achieved (1 Tim 2:3-6). His perfect love longs to cast out all our fear (1 John 4:18).

The cross of Christ is thus the fullest expression of God's love that has ever been or ever will be. Not any nor all of the delights of heaven will express God's love more fully than the giving of his Son at Calvary. In that sense this is God's last message; he has nothing more powerful or more glorious with which to win our faith and love.

The question is whether we can recognize God's love when we see it. Sheep, humble creatures though they are, can instinctively recognize the love and care of a genuine shepherd when they encounter it. 'I am the good shepherd,' says Christ; 'The good shepherd lays down his life for the sheep' (John 10:11). 'By this we know love,' says the Apostle John (1 John 3:16), 'that he laid down his life for us.' 'I am the good shepherd,' says Christ again, 'I know my own and my own know me . . . and I lay down my life for the sheep. . . . For this reason the Father loves me, because I lay down my life' (John 10:14-17).

The question, therefore, is: 'Is this Jesus, crucified and dying on the cross for us (so he says)—is this Jesus the Son of God?' The question is unique. No other religious leader or founder of a world religion will ever stand before you, and addressing himself directly to your heart, say: 'I am your Creator. And because I am your Creator, I love you as you are, in spite of your sin. And the evidence is this: I personally died for you.'

Christ's claim, then, is stupendous. But there is still more evidence to show that it is true.

The evidence supplied by Christ's resurrection

It is common knowledge that the resurrection of Jesus Christ is central to Christianity. It is also clear from the New Testament that the resurrection of Christ and his ascension to heaven were not difficult theological doctrines which the early Christians had to struggle to believe. They were two mighty events which unleashed enormous power that transformed the early disciples from frightened people into irrepressible preachers of the gospel. Far from being a strain upon their faith, Christ's resurrection increased it a thousand-fold. It led them into an experience of the reality of the living God such as they had never known before. Listen to how they spoke:

> Through [Christ you] are believers in God, who raised
> him from the dead and gave him glory, so that your
> faith and hope are in God. (1 Pet 1:21)

Their hope was vastly increased as well. Without God, death is the end of all hope, the final indignity to the body, and the final absurdity and frustration that ends all struggle for progress. But the resurrection of Christ changed all that. Says the Apostle Peter:

> According to [God's] great mercy, he has caused us to
> be born again to a living hope through the resurrec-
> tion of Jesus Christ from the dead, to an inheritance
> that is imperishable, undefiled, and unfading, kept in
> heaven for you. (1 Pet 1:3–4)

The Christians very soon saw that the resurrection of the man, Jesus Christ, opened the doorway into eternal glory for all redeemed mankind. Christ's resurrection was, therefore, the prototype and promise of their own resurrection (1 Cor 15:20–23).

Moreover, the resurrection of Christ produced a remarkable phenomenon: the early Christians, even those who had never seen Jesus, actually loved him. Listen to how they talked:

> Though you have not seen him [Jesus Christ], you love him. Though you do not now see him, you believe in him and rejoice with joy that is inexpressible and filled with glory. (1 Pet 1:8)

If anyone were to say, 'I love Bach', you would take him to mean 'I love his music', not 'I love Bach personally'. No one would say the latter—it would not make sense. Bach is dead; and you cannot love a dead person. A widow will normally say: 'I loved my husband', but not 'I love my husband'.

But that is how all Christians speak about Christ. To them Jesus is not just a historical figure, a moral teacher from the past—he is a living person. Though they have never seen him, they love him, talk to him (in prayer), listen to him speak personally to them (through the Bible), sing to him, worship him and, by his power, live their lives to please him. That is the kind of faith that the reality of the resurrection produces.

'But it is not necessarily a reality,' says someone. 'All this experience occurs in people who first assume that the resurrection of Christ is a historical fact. They persuade themselves that Jesus is alive, form an idealized mental picture of him, and fall in love with the picture. Surely it is pure subjective fantasy. For what objective, historical evidence is there that Jesus actually rose from the dead?'

The answer is: much, very powerful, cumulative evidence of various kinds from a number of different sources. We can only give samples here.

The evidence of the empty tomb: It is quite clear from the records of the New Testament that the first visitors to the tomb of Christ, on the Sunday after he was buried, expected to find his body still in the tomb. They had come with spices to embalm the body, intending by that process to preserve the dead body as long as they could. When they reported to the apostles that they had found the grave empty, the apostles were astonished; and John and Peter immediately ran to the sepulchre to try to discover what had actually happened (John 20:1-10). They tell us what they found. The grave was not exactly empty. The body was gone, but the grave clothes which had been wrapped around the body after the manner of a Jewish burial were still there in the position which they had occupied when the body was still inside them, except that they were now lying flat. The cloths which had been wound round the head were lying slightly apart from the other clothes on the shallow ledge of the tomb which was designed as a cushion to support the corpse's head.

These two disciples tell us that it was this evidence that first made them believe that Jesus must have risen from the dead: the body had come through the clothes leaving them undisturbed. What other explanation could there have been? They knew that none of the other apostles had removed the body; nor could they nor anybody else have done so since the authorities had posted a guard of Roman soldiers round the tomb precisely for this purpose—to prevent anyone stealing the body and faking a resurrection.

It was the soldiers who, on finding that the body was no longer there, set going the rumour that the disciples had come and stolen the body away while they slept (Matt 27:62-66; 28:11-15). But this account of it is, on the face of it, incredible—how could they have seen what happened if they were asleep? But at a deeper level, it is difficult to believe that some disciples got past the guards, removed the heavy gravestone at the tomb entrance, stole the body, hid it away, and then deliberately concocted the lie that Jesus had risen from the dead. It is difficult to believe this for the following two reasons.

The behaviour of the apostles under pressure: Charles Colson was one of President Nixon's aides who concocted a fraudulent story to cover up the President's criminal act in raiding the premises of his political opponents—the so-called Watergate affair. For a while these tough men stuck to their false story. But when pressure mounted, and severe punishment threatened, one after the other betrayed their colleagues and confessed the truth. They found they could not suffer for a lie which they themselves had invented.

From his own experience Colson drew this conclusion. The apostles were politically and diplomatically unsophisticated men. If their story of the resurrection was a lie of their own invention, then when tremendous pressure came on them, as it very soon did, they could not have maintained solidarity: one or other of them would have broken down and confessed that the whole thing was a fraud. But none of them did, not even when they saw many people persecuted and executed for innocently believing their story of the resurrection, nor even when they themselves suffered martyrdom for it.

Yet suppose we admit that they could have maintained solidarity under pressure, how would their story ever have convinced a man like Saul of Tarsus?

The witness of Saul of Tarsus: It is often said that the evidence for Christ's resurrection is seriously weakened by the fact that it all comes from Christians. No non-Christian, so it is claimed, ever testifies that Jesus rose from the dead. Well, of course not. All non-Christians who become convinced of Christ's resurrection naturally become Christians. But the point to grasp is that they were not Christians before they became convinced of his resurrection; and it was his resurrection that convinced them.

A famous case in point is Saul of Tarsus. Before his conversion he not only refused to believe in Jesus and his reported resurrection: he vigorously persecuted all who did. Now the eventual conversion of Saul of Tarsus is an unquestionable historical event. The world bears the marks of its impact still. What, then, caused his conversion? The living, risen, Christ, says Saul, whom he thought to be dead and buried, encountered him on the Damascus road (Acts 9).

Someone might argue that Saul was a very special case. But he was not the only one to be convinced of the resurrection by personal experience of the risen Christ.

The behaviour of the early Christian women: The first people to visit Christ's tomb on the third day were certain Christian women who came to embalm the body. Left to themselves, they would doubtless have turned the tomb into a shrine and a place of pilgrimage, as has been done for many other religious leaders, and indeed as later, superstitious generations in Christendom have done. But these women did not do so. They, and all the early Christians, virtually abandoned the tomb. Why? Because they found it empty, and then they met the Lord Jesus himself, risen from the dead. No one makes a shrine around someone who is alive! (Matt 28:1-10; John 20:11-18).

The testimony of eye-witnesses: The First Epistle to the Corinthians is one of Paul's earlier letters. In 15:3-8 he summarizes the gospel. It includes not only the proclamation that Christ rose from the dead on the third day, but a list of eyewitnesses who had actually seen Christ after his resurrection. This list is not meant to be exhaustive; but it shows that people of widely different personality types were eyewitnesses. The circumstances in which they saw the risen Christ were likewise varied: some people were alone; some in small groups; others in a group of more than 500. We learn elsewhere that Christ appeared to some people at evening behind closed doors (John 20:19-23), to others in broad daylight on a mountain side (Matt 28:16-20), and to yet others in the morning at a lakeside by their fishing boats (John 21), and to still others on a journey (Luke 24). It would be difficult to argue that all these varied personalities were victims of hallucination or mass hypnotism.

Now there is much more such historical evidence that could be quoted. But we ought to consider another objection: 'According to the New Testament, the apostles had to physically see and touch the risen Christ, before they were prepared to believe in his resurrection. How then can you expect me to believe, unless I too can see and touch him?'

The objection is understandable; but it is not so reasonable as might first appear. Let's use an analogy. Suppose that I come from a very undeveloped country and I have never seen electric lighting. When I visit your apartment, you say: 'Press that switch on the wall in your room, and a light will come on.' I ask: 'How is that possible?' You reply: 'The light is produced by electricity which comes from a building called a power station miles away.' I ask: 'Have you seen this electricity?' 'No,' you say. 'Have you seen the power station?' 'I have never been there', you admit. I enquire, 'Why then do you believe in this power station and this electricity, whatever it is?' You patiently explain: 'When we first moved into the apartment, a man visited us who said he came from the power station. He explained that our apartment was at that time disconnected from the electricity supply, but he was going back to the power station and would connect us. The electricity would then flow; and if we pressed the switch, the light would come on. We took him at his word, pressed the switch, and the light came on. So now go to your room, press the switch, and the light will come on in your room, too.'

Suppose I replied, 'No, I am not prepared to do that. I might deceive myself into imagining I saw the light come on. I insist on first seeing the man from the power station myself, just like you did before you pressed your switch.'

You would probably think I was crazy.

Now the apostles tell us that Jesus informed them, both before he died, and after he rose from the dead, that he was deliberately going to leave them. He was returning to the Father from whom he had come, so that he might send the Holy Spirit to them (John 16:7-14, 28). They were to wait in Jerusalem certain days and then they would receive the Holy Spirit. He then left them and ascended into heaven (Acts 1:4-9). They took him at his word, waited as they were told, and then received the Holy Spirit, and with him light, peace, and power to live a life in daily fellowship with God.

They then told their contemporaries that if they repented of their sin and believed in Christ, they too would receive the Holy Spirit (Acts 2:38). They would not, and they could not, see the Holy Spirit; but they would experience his light and power. The apostles say the same to us today. They themselves had to see the risen Christ in order to be able to assure the world that he was the same Jesus with whom they had lived for three years (Acts 1:21-22). But we do not need to see 'the man from the power station'. We can discover that he is really alive without that. Press the switch of repentance and faith, and the light and power of his Spirit will come on in our hearts.

We have another safeguard against the danger of mere subjectivism. The resurrection of Jesus was not the resurrection of just any man. The Old Testament Scriptures were God's book of instructions telling people what they were to expect the Saviour to do when he came. He would first die as God's appointed sacrifice for the sins of the world. God would then validate that sacrifice by raising him from the dead (Isa 53:4-6, 10-12). Jesus claimed to be that Saviour. That is why the Christian gospel is not merely that Christ died and rose again. It is that 'Christ died for our sins *according to the Scriptures* ... and that he rose again the third day *according to the Scriptures*' (1 Cor 15:3-4). Read these Scriptures; and then prove by the appropriate action that this gospel is true.

CHAPTER 11

Faith

A Question of Whom You Trust

So far in the chapters on the concept of faith we have been considering the grounds on which we are invited to believe the fact that Jesus is the Christ, the Son of God. The Bible honestly warns us that believing this fact can involve people in considerable suffering. Faith needs, then, to be very clear headed as to what exactly it believes. If Jesus really is the Son of God, Son of the owner of the universe, Creator and possessor of all things, then any loss or suffering we incur for his sake is as nothing compared to what we have in him. On the other hand, if Jesus is not the Son of God, we would be foolish to incur any suffering or loss for his sake.

Again, some people, for instance, will say, 'We believe in Christ and all other religions as well.' But such broadmindedness is dangerously illogical. Faith in Christ, according to the New Testament, means believing that 'There is one God, and there is one mediator between God and men, the man Christ Jesus, who gave himself as a ransom for all' (1 Tim 2:5-6). It means believing that 'there is salvation in no one else, for there is no other name ... by which we must be saved' (Acts 4:12). It means believing that his sacrifice for sin is all-sufficient. No other is possible, no other is needed (Heb 10:11-12). To claim to believe in Christ as Saviour and in some other saviour as well is not faith (nor intelligence either) but unbelief.

But true Christian faith not only means believing certain facts: it also means believing in, trusting, and committing oneself entirely to, a person, that is, to our Lord Jesus Christ. Unfortunately there are many people who believe the fact that Jesus is the Son of God and the Saviour of the world, but who nevertheless have not committed themselves entirely to him to save them personally. Strangely enough, this is the temptation to which religious people (though, of course, not only they) are especially prone.

Some feel no need to commit themselves personally to Christ. They are confident that their own record of honest attempts to keep God's law and their regular use of the Church's sacraments will see them through. They seem oblivious to God's stern reminder that all who take their stand on the law are under a curse (Gal 3:10-12).

Some are afraid to commit themselves solely to Christ for salvation. They feel that Christ does his part in saving us, but that we have to do a considerable amount as well to save ourselves. This they find to be quite hard work, and even so they are never completely sure that it will be enough to save them in the end. They need to listen again to the New Testament's liberating words:

> For we hold that one is justified by faith apart from
> works of the law. .... And to the one who does not
> work but believes in him who justifies the ungodly, his
> faith is counted as righteousness. (Rom 3:28; 4:5)

When a lifeguard swims out to rescue a man who is in danger of drowning, he will not necessarily attempt to save the man the moment he reaches him. The reason is that the man in his panic is liable to keep struggling to save himself, grab hold of the life-saver and thus make rescue impossible. So the rescuer will swim round at a little distance, until the man is exhausted and gives up struggling to save himself. Then at that point the rescuer will close in with him and do all the saving. Very often Christ has to act like that. He waits until people have discovered that there is nothing they can do to save themselves; and then he presents himself to them as the Saviour who does all the saving.

Other people have a different problem. Realizing that salvation is by faith, they try hard to believe. But in spite of all their efforts to believe, they feel that their faith is not strong enough; and so they have no assurance of salvation. Their mistake is that, consciously or unconsciously, they are regarding faith as a meritorious work, which will qualify for salvation only if it is strong enough. But salvation is a genuine gift. Faith does not merit it. Faith is the outstretched, trembling hand of a bankrupt beggar that simply takes the unearned and undeserved gift (Eph 2:8–9).

A little child will happily fall asleep in its mother's arms, trusting its mother to keep it safe. The child's faith in its mother does not merit or earn its mother's care, nor does the child have to work hard in order to enjoy the security which its mother's love freely gives it.

On the other hand, faith is not mere self-confidence. Some people, for instance, will say: 'I have great faith that if I do the best I can, God will in the end have mercy on me and grant me salvation.' But such faith is not what the New Testament means by faith, for its confidence is based, not on God and what God says, but upon the speaker's own opinions. Such confidence is, in fact, dangerously misplaced.

Suppose a mother buys medicine for her child. The label says that the medicine must only be applied externally: it is poisonous if taken internally. But the mother does not bother to read the label and makes her child drink a large spoonful of the medicine. She feels confident that the medicine will do the child good. But will it? Of course not. The child might well die. Confidence, then, is valid only when it is based on God, and what God says.

And here is another important distinction: faith is not feelings. Many people (though not everyone), when they first trust Christ and receive complete forgiveness of sins and assurance of salvation, experience great emotional relief, and feelings of exhilaration. That is good. But after a while these feelings naturally subside. At that point, if their faith is relying on their feelings instead of on Christ, they can come to think that perhaps they have lost their salvation, or perhaps never really had it at all. We must not, then, confuse faith with feelings. Faith in God can in fact sometimes cause us feelings of sorrow and pain, as for instance when God's word convicts us of our wrong behaviour and the damage it has caused, or when we find that God requires us to give up unethical practices that we have used to make money, or when we have to suffer abuse or persecution for being believers. We must therefore make God's word, and not our feelings, our ultimate guide.

Suppose a child lives in an apartment on the fifth floor of a building. Her apartment catches fire. Presently a fireman appears outside her window on top of a long ladder. He steps inside and tells her that she must let him carry her down the ladder. She consents and entrusts herself to him. But when she looks down and sees the ground far below, she is filled with feelings of fear. But her feelings make no difference to her security. The fireman holds her in his iron-like grip, and brings her safely down. So once we put our faith in Christ as Saviour, it is his strength and faithfulness that guarantee our salvation. Our feelings are irrelevant to our security.

Faith involves making a moral judgment

Someone may say: 'If I trust Christ to give me the security of eternal life, how shall I know that I have got it?' Here is the New Testament's answer to his question:

> If we receive the testimony of men, the testimony of God is greater, for this is the testimony of God that he has borne concerning his Son. Whoever believes in the Son of God has the testimony in himself. Whoever does not believe God has made him a liar, because he has not believed in the testimony that God has borne concerning his Son. And this is the testimony, that God

gave us eternal life, and this life is in his Son. Whoever
has the Son has life; whoever does not have the Son of
God does not have life. I write these things to you who
believe in the name of the Son of God that you may
know that you have eternal life. (1 John 5:9-13)

This passage of God's own Word tells us that a believer in
Christ can be utterly sure that he has eternal life, on two
grounds.

1. Because God says so! And not to believe God when he
tells us something is to imply that he is a liar.

God's Word is plain, simple, and straightforward:

And this is the testimony, that God gave us eternal life,
and this life is in his Son. (1 John 5:11)

That ought to settle it for every believer.

Suppose the first time I met you I asked you what your
name was, and you replied, 'Mary.' And suppose at that
moment someone else came and said to me, 'What is that
lady's name?' And I replied: 'I don't know. She says it is Mary.
But I cannot be sure.' How would you feel? You would be
highly indignant, for by refusing to believe what you told
me, I would be implying that you were a liar. I would be
impugning your moral character. That would be serious;
but not anywhere near so serious as refusing to believe
what God says and so impugning God's character. Believing
God, therefore, involves making a judgment as to his moral
character: is he trustworthy? Does he tell the truth?

Man's whole trouble began when, in the garden of Eden,
Satan artfully deceived him into questioning and doubting

God's word and so began his alienation from God (Gen 3:1–7). That alienation is removed when a man in repentance and faith puts his absolute trust in the word and character of God who cannot lie.

2. Because 'he who believes has the witness in himself' (1 John 5:10). Suppose you were ill, and a doctor offered you some medicine, and said, 'Take this medicine, and it will cure you.' You would have to decide first whether to believe him or not. Was he properly qualified? Could you be sure that what he was offering you was good medicine and not poison? But suppose you decided that he was a well-qualified doctor and a man of trustworthy character. Then you would take the medicine; and as the medicine took effect and cured you, you would have the evidence within yourself that the doctor was true and the medicine was good.

In the same way God offers to give us eternal life as a gift. If we believe him, we shall come to realize that we have this gift, first because God tells us so, but then also because of the actual changes it will make within us.

The life of faith

Earlier in this chapter we learned that, when it comes to receiving salvation, faith is the opposite of works: 'by faith' means 'not by works'. Now we are to learn that true faith leads to, or produces, works. Indeed, faith that does not produce works is not genuine faith. If this sounds contradictory, consider the following analogy.

A farmer has such a weak heart that he can no longer work. A heart surgeon friend of his, offers to perform a

heart transplant operation free of charge. Both the operation and the new heart are to be accepted as a free gift.
The farmer believes the surgeon, commits himself to him,
the operation is performed, and the new heart is success-
fully installed. As a result, the farmer finds himself full of
new life and energy, and gladly works, not in order to get
the new heart, but because he has got it.

So God gives to everyone who believes in Christ the
spiritual gift of a new heart. It is a genuinely free gift, not
earned by working. But with the new heart comes new
life, energies, goals, motives, and desires which delight to
spend themselves in the service of Christ (see Ezek 11:19-20).
This indeed is the objective of salvation, as Paul points out
to his converts. The verses in which he reminds them that
they have been saved by faith without works are followed
by verses which tell them that they 'have been created in
Christ Jesus for good works which God prepared before-
hand that they should walk in them' (Eph 2:8-10).

As well, every step along life's path will be a call to
the continuous exercise of faith; and faith, like muscles,
will grow stronger with exercise. Faith will enable the
believer to live and work according to Christ's commandments. Faith will strengthen him to follow the example
of the great heroes of faith of all ages, who have done
great exploits, or endured great suffering for God's sake
(see Heb 11).

Furthermore, God will allow faith to be tested, sometimes severely, so that it may be demonstrated to be
genuine. It is thus purified like gold is heated to cleanse
away the dross, and make the gold more valuable (1 Pet
1:6-7). But the believer is assured that God will not allow

him to be tempted beyond what he is able to bear (1 Cor 10:13). Indeed Christ by his intercession will maintain his faith, and, if it falters, restore it, as he did for Peter long ago (Luke 22:31–32; Heb 7:25).

Faith will also empower the believer to hold fast the fundamental doctrines of Christianity which the New Testament calls 'the faith'. As Paul wrote, we are to 'fight the good fight of the faith' (1 Tim 6:12–16). And faith will most assuredly reap its final reward:

> I have fought the good fight, I have finished the race, I have kept the faith. Henceforth there is laid up for me the crown of righteousness, which the Lord, the righteous judge, will award to me on that Day, and not only to me but also to all who have loved his appearing. (2 Tim 4:7–8)

CHAPTER 12

Sanctification

Like Father, Like Son

The term *sanctification* denotes the process by which God turns sinful people into saints. Now the New Testament in general is full of surprises for those who are not already familiar with it; but nowhere more so than in its usage of the word 'saint'. In popular speech the title 'Saint' is commonly used as an honorific in referring to the Christian apostles, St. Peter, St. Paul, etc.; and it is also applied to people who are thought to have attained to an advanced degree of holiness during their lifetime, such as, for instance, St. Francis or St. Sophia.

But the New Testament usage is markedly different from this. Never once in the original text (the headings to the Epistles are not original: they are later additions) are individual apostles referred to as St. Peter, or St. Paul, etc., though the apostles and prophets as a whole are referred to occasionally as the 'holy apostles and prophets' (Eph 3:5;

2 Pet 3:2). On the other hand, *all* Christians without exception are constantly referred to as saints. When it says in Acts 9:32, for instance, that Peter 'went ... to the saints in Lydda', it does not mean that he went to visit only a select few of the Christians: 'the saints' is the normal New Testament way of referring to all the Christians in a locality.

Even more surprising, Paul's letter to the church at Corinth shows that much in its members' behaviour was unworthy. Yet in his opening remarks he addresses all its members as 'those sanctified in Christ Jesus, called to be saints' (1 Cor 1:2).

Such language, however, is not superficial, diplomatic flattery. It springs from the heart of the gospel. Some of the Corinthian believers had formerly been extremely immoral; all had been sinful; many of them were still spiritually weak and immature. 'But,' says Paul, 'you were washed, you were sanctified, you were justified in the name of the Lord Jesus Christ and by the Spirit of our God' (1 Cor 6:11). In talking like this, the New Testament does not imply that people who have thus been sanctified and become saints have no need to constantly make progress in practical holiness. But it does assert that such are the merits of Christ's sacrifice that all who put their faith in him are then and there declared by God to be truly sanctified and are rightly called saints.

To see how this can be, let us start with a definition of 'holiness'. Sanctification has two sides to it:

1. On the one side, it involves separation from uncleanness and impurity, in other words purification. Holiness demands that we actively avoid doing certain things.

2. On the other side, it means separation to God and to his service, in other words, consecration. Holiness demands that we actively pursue doing certain other things.

Both are well brought out in Hebrews 9:13-14. Here the writer is contrasting the ancient Jewish means of sanctification with those of Christianity. He associates sanctification both with purification from defilement and with consecration to the service of God:

> For if the blood of goats and bulls, and the sprinkling of defiled persons with the ashes of a heifer, sanctify for the purification of the flesh, how much more will the blood of Christ, who through the eternal Spirit offered himself without blemish to God, purify our conscience from dead works to serve the living God. (Heb 9:13-14)

Next we should notice that the New Testament speaks of 'sanctification' as being achieved in three stages: initial, progressive, and final. We will consider the first of these stages here and the second and third stages in our next chapter.

Initial sanctification

First, notice how initial sanctification is said to be brought about by:

1. *The offering of the body of Christ:*

> Consequently, when Christ came into the world, he said, 'Sacrifices and offerings you have not desired, but a body have you prepared for me' ... Then I said,

"Behold, I have come to do your will, O God"' . . . And by
that will we have been sanctified through the offering
of the body of Jesus Christ once for all. (Heb 10:5, 7, 10)

It is not, then, by our own efforts to keep God's law and
to do his will that we make ourselves saints. All our efforts to
that end would come disastrously short of the purity, holiness, and devotion that God requires. The gospel is that we
are made holy and acceptable to God by what someone else—
namely Christ—has done. It was God's will that he should
offer his body as a sinless sacrifice and substitute for us; and
he did that once for all when he offered himself to God on
the cross. It is that sacrifice, and not our efforts, that make
us, in spite of all our failings, acceptable to God.

2. *The blood of Christ:* (see Heb 9:13–14, p. 112.) No one
can serve the living God acceptably while his conscience
is defiled by guilt. Guilt casts a shadow and an aura of
decay and morbidity over the whole man and over all
that he does. No increase of religious activity on our part
can dispel that defilement. Nor can religious ceremonies
and ritual washings (see Matt 15). But what we cannot
do, the blood of Christ can: for 'the blood of Jesus [God's
Son] cleanses us from all sin' (1 John 1:7). It cleanses our
conscience and sets us free to serve the living God.

The blood of Christ effects, then, the one side of sanctification, the element of purification from defilement. What
is it that effects the other side of sanctification, that is, the
element of consecration to God?

On God's part, it is effected by the work of the Holy Spirit
in our hearts, convicting us of sin, drawing us to the Saviour,
revealing to us God's way of salvation, and implanting

113

within us, by his regenerating power, the very life of God with all the necessary potential for developing a holy life.

> [God] saved us . . . by the washing of regeneration and renewal of the Holy Spirit. (Titus 3:5)

> According to the foreknowledge of God the Father, in the sanctification of the Spirit, for obedience to Jesus Christ and for sprinkling with his blood. (1 Pet 1:2)

And on our part both elements of sanctification are effected in our hearts by faith:

> And God, who knows the heart, bore witness to them, by giving them the Holy Spirit just as he did to us, and he made no distinction between us [Jews] and them [Gentiles], having cleansed their hearts by faith. (Acts 15:8–9)

When, in response to the working of the Holy Spirit in our hearts, we abandon faith in ourselves for salvation and put our trust solely in God and in Christ's sacrifice, it produces a fundamental change in the orientation of our hearts. Gone is the old alienation and enmity against God. Gone is our former independence and disregard of God. In their place the Holy Spirit makes us conscious of God's love towards us: 'because God's love has been poured into our hearts through the Holy Spirit' (Rom 5:5). He makes us aware that we have now become children of God, sharing the life and nature of our Father so that instinctively and naturally we address him as Abba Father (Rom 8:14–17), and sense both the duty and the possibility of being holy as our Father is holy (1 Pet 1:14-16).

Simultaneously we find that 'through him [Christ] we both [that is, both Jews and Gentiles] have access in one Spirit to the Father' (Eph 2:18). This, of course, was not always so. In the centuries before the birth, life, and death of Christ, the sacrifices which the Israelites offered for their sins were only symbols. They could not take away their sins, since they did not actually pay the penalty of those sins. In consequence, the ordinary Israelite was allowed to enter only the outer court of God's earthly tabernacle or temple. The priests entered the Holy Place but no further. Only the high priest was permitted to enter the Most Holy Place where stood God's throne.

But now that Christ has come and offered a perfect sacrifice for sin, all that has changed. Christ has perfected forever those who are being sanctified (Heb 10:14). All believers, therefore, and not just a specially ordained few, have—even now, here on earth—right of spiritual access into the Most Holy Place of God's presence in heaven itself, and confidence thus to enter and draw near to God. Hebrews 10:19-22 explains how that can be: Jesus has opened the way for them through his blood, and every believer has had his heart sprinkled by that blood to cleanse it from a guilty conscience and his body, metaphorically speaking, bathed with pure water (compare John 13:6-11).

With the constant enjoyment of this access into the presence of God, believers then become aware that they have been made priests to God, all of them, consecrated to the service of God by the blood of Christ (Rev 1:5-6; 5:9-10).

So the Apostle Peter informs all his fellow-believers:

> You yourselves ... are being built up as a spiritual
> house, to be a holy priesthood, to offer spiritual sac-
> rifices acceptable to God through Jesus Christ. ... But
> you are a chosen race, a royal priesthood, a holy nation,
> a people for his own possession, that you may pro-
> claim the excellencies of him who called you out of
> darkness into his marvellous light. Once you were not
> a people, but now you are God's people; once you had
> not received mercy, but now you have received mercy.
> (1 Pet 2:5, 9-10)

All this understandably produces in believers a deep-
lying love for God. 'We love', says the Apostle John, 'because
he first loved us' (1 John 4:19). This in turn becomes their
motivation for gladly devoting their lives at home, in
school, in the factory or office, or on the farm, to the service of God. 'I appeal to you therefore, brothers,' says the
Apostle Paul 'by the mercies of God, to present your bodies as a living sacrifice, holy and acceptable to God, which
is your reasonable service. And do not be conformed to
this world; but be transformed by the renewing of your
mind that you may prove what is the good and acceptable
and perfect will of God' (Rom 12:1-2 own trans.).

This appeal is based on an inescapable logic. Several
passages in the New Testament spell it out. Here is one
example:

> For the love of Christ controls us, because we have
> concluded this: that one has died for all, therefore

all have died; and he died for all, that those who live
might no longer live for themselves but for him who
for their sake died and was raised. (2 Cor 5:14–15)

Another passage adds a further motive for leading a
holy life:

Or do you not know that your body is a temple of the
Holy Spirit within you, whom you have from God? You
are not your own, for you were bought with a price.
So glorify God in your body. (1 Cor 6:19–20)

We notice here the same logic as before: a believer
has been redeemed at the cost of the blood of Christ.
From now on neither the believer nor even his physical body belongs to himself. Both belong to Christ. But
more: through Christ's redemption the believer's body has
been constituted a temple of the Holy Spirit, for when
he believed, God put his Holy Spirit within him. The very
presence of the Holy Spirit therefore, in a believer's body,
makes it holy and consecrates it as a dwelling place of
God. It is this awesome fact that lays upon the believer
the bounden duty to glorify God in his body, and to avoid
defiling what has now become the Holy Spirit's temple.

The order of events here is both striking and instructive.
The believer is not told that if he first cleans up his life sufficiently, the Holy Spirit will perhaps condescend to come
and make his body his temple. It is the other way around.
Christ, by his sacrifice and blood, has already cleansed and
sanctified the believer's body and made it into a temple of
the Holy Spirit. Since that is already a fact, the believer is

now responsible, and motivated, to abstain from behaviour that would defile his body.

Let us sum up what we have learned so far. Initial sanctification, as we have called it, is not something that we have to attain to or accomplish by our own efforts to lead a holy life. It is something that God bestows on us from the very moment that we put our faith in Christ:

> And because of him [God] you are in Christ Jesus, who became to us wisdom from God, righteousness and sanctification and redemption. (1 Cor 1:30)

This initial sanctification constitutes every believer a saint. It gives every believer immediate and direct access to the Father. It consecrates every believer as a priest to God, to offer to God spiritual sacrifices and to tell out to others God's redeeming love and grace. It makes every believer's body a holy temple in which the Spirit of God resides. It creates in every believer the instinctive awareness that he is now a child of God, with his Father's own life within him, and therefore with all the necessary potential for being holy as the Father is holy. And it produces in all believers a love and gratitude to God and to Christ that motivate them to live a life of devotion to the divine persons. And not only a love to God and Christ, but also a love to all those, of whatever race or nationality, that have likewise been begotten of the same Father (1 John 5:1).

But at this point someone may well object: 'This makes it sound all too easy. Does not the Bible itself represent the Christian life as a life of struggle, striving, and warfare?' Yes, it does and we will consider that in our next chapter.

CHAPTER 13

Sanctification

Sonship Not Slavery

In our last chapter we studied initial sanctification; now we must investigate what the New Testament means first by progressive sanctification and then by final sanctification.

Progressive sanctification

The first thing to notice here is the straightforward fact: the Bible insists that while people are sanctified and constituted genuine saints the moment they put their faith in Christ (as we saw in our last chapter), they still need constantly thereafter to 'cleanse [themselves] from every defilement of body and spirit, bringing holiness to completion in the fear of God' (2 Cor 7:1). Noticing this will save us from a common mistake. The Bible does indeed teach that a man is justified by faith, solely by God's grace and not on the grounds of his works or of his spiritual attainment either before or after his conversion (Rom 3:19-28). But that does not mean, as so many have mistakenly supposed, that once justified by grace a man is free to live a sinful life. Listen to Paul's double protest:

> What shall we say then? Are we to continue in sin that grace may abound? By no means! . . . What then? Are we to sin because we are not under law but under grace? By no means! (Rom 6:1-2, 15)

Moreover, Paul makes it indisputably clear that when Christ undertakes to save us, he not only forgives our sins, he insists on making us ever more holy. True conversion, so he reminded his converts (Eph 4:17-24), involved agreeing with Christ decisively right from the start 'to put off your old self', that is one's old sinful lifestyle, and 'to put on the new self', that is the lifestyle that God has himself designed for those that have been reconciled to him. This would mean to actively persist in that 'putting off' and 'putting on' for the rest of one's life. In other words, for a man who has been justified by faith solely by the grace of God and not by his works, progressive sanctification is not optional. According to the New Testament, it is obligatory. Indeed anyone who rejects this obligation is not a true believer.

But now notice by what means this progressive sanctification is to be achieved.

There are basically two ways of going about it. Both ways involve positive action and perseverance on our part. But the one way is wrong, and the other way is right. One way is the way of a slave; it is ineffective and leads to frustration and despair (see Rom 7:7-25). The other way is the way of God's free-born sons and it leads them into ever deepening fellowship with their Father and into ever increasing conformity to his way of thinking and behaving (see Matt 5:43-48). It is well summed up in Romans 8:13-17:

> For if you live according to the flesh you will die, but if by the Spirit you put to death the deeds of the body, you will live. For all who are led by the Spirit of God are sons of God. For you did not receive the spirit of slavery to fall back into fear, but you have received the Spirit of adoption as sons, by whom we cry, 'Abba! Father!' The Spirit himself bears witness with our spirit that we are children of God, and if children, then heirs—heirs of God and fellow heirs with Christ, provided we suffer with him in order that we may also be glorified with him.

The trouble with the wrong method is this: it sees that God's law is holy, just, and good; that its commands are reasonable; and that the benefits that come from fulfilling the law are altogether desirable (Rom 7:12). But from that it jumps to the conclusion that the New Testament's recipe for progressive sanctification will be simply this: 'Here is God's law; here are the ten commandments; here is Christ's Sermon on the Mount; make up your mind, brace your will, do your best to keep them, and you will become more and more holy.'

This view, however, overlooks three important facts:

1. Human beings have been so damaged, enfeebled, and corrupted by sin that, try as they will, they cannot

keep God's law. They may delight in the law of God, serve it intellectually, and determine with all their will power to keep it, as the Apostle Paul confesses he once did (Rom 7:15, 18–19, 22, 25). But they will find with Paul that they invariably fail to carry it out fully in practice. Indeed, they will discover that deep within them there is a powerful opposition to the keeping of God's law, which acts with all the determination of a military campaign to maintain sin's domination (Rom 7:23).

2. In this situation, God's law, good as it is in itself, can give the person no help. It is, as the Bible puts it, unable to achieve success, because of the weakness of the flesh (Rom 8:3). Indeed, by concentrating the person's mind on his sinful tendencies it often reinforces them (Rom 7:7–8); and by emphasizing the person's constant failures, it undermines his strength to overcome them (Rom 7:21–24).

3. And then there is a third thing, which we easily forget. God's law instructs us how we ought to behave, but it is more than that. It is command *plus penalty for failure* or disobedience; and its ultimate penalty is rejection by God. A man has only to fail once, and no amount of success after that can compensate for the failure or cancel the penalty. In a system where the demand is for constant perfection, there can be no excess goodness to make up for any imperfection.

To help grasp the practical implications of this, let us construct an analogy. Suppose a sanatorium for tuberculosis sufferers is situated in a remote valley. At the further end of the valley is a nuclear power station and it begins to leak its invisible but lethal radiation. The government therefore advises the patients to flee for their lives. Unfortunately the only exit is by four mountain passes rising to 4,000 meters; and the government informs the patients that not until they have cleared the whole mountain range will they be safe from the radiation.

The government's advice is of course sound; any sensible person would want to follow it. But it so happens that the government cannot, or else does not, give the patients any help to cross the range: no helicopters, no buses, not even horses or mules. They just have to do their best on foot. Driven by fear of fatal radiation they might make an heroic effort to escape, but their illness would render their progress pitifully slow until it became obvious that they had virtually no hope of crossing the range before they succumbed either to their original illness, or to the elements, or to the effects of radiation.

But suppose in addition the government told them that they must cross all four mountains within three days. Any who took longer would be so badly irradiated that they would be a danger to other people. They would therefore be shot on sight as soon as they emerged. In their weak state they would find that crossing the first two mountains took them more than the permitted three days. What then would be the point of their struggling to cross the next two, if at the end, in spite of all their efforts, they must face the death penalty?

Every fibre in our being protests that God cannot be like this; and of course he isn't! His way of achieving progressive holiness is not by simply giving people his law and commanding them to do their best to keep it. If it were, their plight would be no better than that of the patients. Both God's love and his realism have moved him to provide an altogether different way.

His first step towards breaking the overpowering stranglehold of sin on their lives has been to remove from them forever the penalty for failing to keep his law perfectly. 'Sin will have no dominion over you, since you are not under law but under grace' (Rom 6:14). Christ by his death has paid that penalty for them once and for all (Rom 6:6–11). Now, therefore, they are free. If they were still 'under the law' and liable to its penalty, one mistake, fall, or sin would be enough to incur the penalty. In which case all attempts to make further progress in sanctification, would be pointless. Sin would thus have conquered and foiled their attempt to escape its dominion.

But now it is not pointless. When in spite of their efforts they sin and fall, they can confess their sin to God, and 'he is faithful and just to forgive [them their] sins and to cleanse [them] from all unrighteousness' (1 John 1:9). And there being no penalty to face either now or in the future, they are free to get up again and struggle on in the path of progressive holiness.

The second step that God has taken to break the mastery of sin is to provide help and power such as the law could never give. 'Likewise, my brothers, you also have died to the law through the body of Christ, so that you may belong to another, to him who has been raised from the dead [that is, Christ], in order that we may bear fruit for God' (Rom 7:4). It is not, we repeat, that God's law is bad, or that its requirements can be ignored. God's purpose is that we should fulfil its requirements (Rom 8:4). But the law itself cannot provide us with the power to do so. The New Testament's answer to this problem, therefore, is what may be called, metaphorically speaking, 'marriage with Christ', or as our passage puts it 'that you may belong to another' (see also 1 Cor 6:16–17).

A woman might read through endless books on physiology and long to have children; but she would have no hope of having any without a husband. So Christ, risen from the dead, becomes a living, loving, spiritual husband to those who trust him, supplying the necessary life and power, so that they 'may bring forth fruit unto God' in the form of progressive holiness.

It is evident that the New Testament does not conceive of this relationship as overpowering a believer's personality, any more than getting married to a husband reduces a woman to a mere machine. A believer still remains a responsible individual. It is he who must be diligent to make progress in holiness (2 Pet 1:1–11), he who must live to please and serve God. But it is no longer a matter of simply reading instructions written in a book, or on tablets of stone as the Ten Commandments were, and then trying to carry them out. That would be what the following passage calls serving 'in the old way of the written code':

> But now we are released from the law . . . so that we serve in the new way of the Spirit and not in the old way of the written code. (Rom 7:6)

The Holy Spirit of God, who had God's laws written down in the Bible as an expression of God's holy character, now lives out those laws as a person in and through the believer. He works within the believer to renew his mind, change his outlook, reorganize his scale of values, empower his will, re-direct his ambition, and oppose his wrong desires. We are told that the Spirit brings strong forces to bear, 'against the flesh . . . to keep you from doing the things you want to do' (see Gal 5:16–24).

This relationship between the believer and Christ through the Holy Spirit, however, is not a matter of vague impressions and nebulous, incomprehensible, and inexpressible visions. Christ will constantly direct his people's minds to God's Word. The New Testament records that as he prayed to his Father for his disciples' progress in sanctification he said: 'Sanctify them in the truth; your word is truth' (John 17:17). The believer, of course, is still able to choose whether he 'sows to his own flesh' or he 'sows to the Spirit' (cf. Gal 6:8). But in his choice he is no longer driven, like a slave under the lash, by fear of the penalty of God's law, but led by the Spirit who makes him instinctively aware that he is a child of the Father, with the Father's love and life and nature within him (Rom 8:14–17). And just like the force generated by a gyro-compass helps maintain an aircraft on its course, so the Holy Spirit's intercessions, alongside the believer's own inner desires, maintain him along the course plotted for him by God, a course that proceeds via his calling and justification to the final goal of his glorification (Rom 8:26–30).

There is no pretence in the Bible that progress along this course is always smooth. When a child of God strays from the path, as children will, or needs some impulse to increase his progress, God as his Father will not hesitate to discipline him. And the discipline can be painful. But it is applied by the Father's love and wisdom so that the believer may the better partake of the Father's holiness (Heb 12:1–13). And the goal is certain and secure. Right from the beginning of the course, the believer is assured that, having been justified by faith, he shall attain the glory of God (Rom 5:1–2).

Final sanctification

From time to time some people have formed the idea that a Christian can be sinlessly perfect in this life. The Bible denies it. As long as we live in this world we all have to admit with Paul:

> Not that I have already obtained this or am already perfect, but I press on to make it my own, because Christ Jesus has made me his own. (Phil 3:12)

The believer's sanctification will be completed at the second coming of Christ. Then the believer shall be physically, morally and spiritually conformed to Christ. And the Bible tells us how:

> Beloved, we are God's children now, and what we will be has not yet appeared; but we know that when he appears we shall be like him, because we shall see him as he is. (1 John 3:2)

CHAPTER 14

The Final Judgment

The Demands of Justice

It is a very interesting fact that children, even at a young age, develop a very strong feeling for what is just and fair, and what is unfair. 'It's not fair', says the child when his younger brother snatches his toy away and his parents allow the younger child to keep it and play with it. 'It's not fair', says the schoolgirl when the teacher blames and punishes her for something which, in fact, she did not do.

Our instinctive sense of justice

Maybe as we get older the intensity of our indignation at injustice gets blunted, for the simple reason that we have witnessed so many instances of it, that we become hardened and cynical. Even so, we can still feel outraged when, for instance, we see someone getting fabulously rich by selling off public property and putting the proceeds into his own pocket. We may resign ourselves to the fact that we ourselves cannot do anything about it; but we still protest: 'It isn't fair'; and our protest carries within it, spoken or unspoken, the feeling that somebody should do something about it: unfairness should not be allowed to continue; cheats, liars, murderers, and all other perpetrators of evil should not be allowed to go unpunished.

And yet history, and our own recent experience, show us that that is precisely what appears to happen. Even governments whose responsibility it is to punish criminals have themselves all too often been guilty of corruption and sometimes of monstrous crimes. Death in the end seems to take all away indiscriminately, the law-abiding and the law-breakers, saints and sinners alike. Must we conclude then that crime and sin, petty and gross injustice, will never be punished; that our sense of right and wrong is a mocking illusion, that our hope of justice will be forever frustrated?

No! According to the Bible, God himself is the author of our sense of right and wrong. The Creator has written his law on our hearts (Rom 2:14–15); and conscience is his internal monitor warning us not to break that law, witnessing to us, when we break it, that we are doing wrong, and filling us, after the bad deed is done, with a sense of guilt.

One day, the New Testament assures us, God will vindicate his law. There will come the final judgment. In this connection another term is also used, the 'second death'. This term denotes what the eternal state will be of those who find themselves condemned at that final judgment.

Then I saw a great white throne and him who was seated on it. From his presence earth and sky fled away, and no place was found for them. And I saw the dead, great and small, standing before the throne, and books were opened. Then another book was opened, which is the book of life. And the dead were judged by what was written in the books, according to what they had done. And the sea gave up the dead who were in it, Death and Hades gave up the dead who were in them, and they were judged, each one of them, according to what they had done. Then Death and Hades were thrown into the lake of fire. This is the second death, the lake of fire. And if anyone's name was not found written in the book of life, he was thrown into the lake of fire. (Rev 20:11–15)

When the final judgment will take place

As far as each individual is concerned, the judgment takes place after death: 'It is appointed for man to die once, and after that comes judgment' (Heb 9:27). But if we ask how long after the individual's death the final judgment comes, the answer is: the final judgment comes after heaven and earth have fled away, that is, at, or after, the end of the world.

Now it is easy to see why that must be so. Sin, once committed, can have a chain reaction that continues long after the person who committed the sin has died. A father, for instance, may through his harsh treatment and love-lessness, injure his young son psychologically. The son, growing up psychologically ill-adjusted, may behave in a hurtful way towards his wife, children, relatives and work mates, who as a result may in turn react reprehensibly.

Likewise the damage and injustice that the great tyrants have done to millions of people did not cease when those tyrants died; it has gone on spreading like ripples on a pond. Not until the whole complicated web of human history is cut off from the loom at the end of the world will it be possible to estimate fully and justly the true significance of any one sin.

The thoroughness of the judgment

The New Testament passage, quoted above, says: 'the books were opened . . . And the dead were judged by what was written in the books' (Rev 20:12). We need not suppose that God's record books are exactly like the books we have on earth: the word 'books' here is a metaphor. But it reminds us that God has a record of everything that every person has ever thought, said and done. God's ability to keep such records should not seem to us incredible. Humans themselves can nowadays make computers with almost limitless memory banks.

The New Testament also reminds us that after death people not only continue to exist, but they will be able to remember their past lives, perhaps in greater detail than they were able to in this life (Luke 16:25). God will judge not only the outward deeds but the secrets of men (Rom 2:16). Just as we can capture our actions on a video and then play them back so that we can in the present see ourselves doing and saying things years ago, so God will be able to play back in front of people's eyes their secret thoughts and open actions from years, or even centuries, ago.

The judgment will therefore be scrupulously fair, since each individual will be judged, our passage says, according to his or her works. No one will be punished, or rewarded, for what someone else did. Moreover the judge (who will be none other than our Lord Jesus Christ: see John 5:22, 27–29), will take into account what knowledge of right and wrong people had or did not have. He himself put it like this:

> And that servant who knew his master's will but did not get ready or act according to his will, will receive a severe beating. But the one who did not know [his Lord's will], and did what deserved a beating, will receive a light beating. (Luke 12:47–48a)

A man may well kill simply because he has been brought up from babyhood in an illiterate tribe who have taught him that killing members of an adjacent tribe is a good and glorious thing. What he does is sinful in God's eyes; but he will not be treated with the same severity as the drug baron who grew up in a country where he was taught that murder is sin, but nonetheless deliberately murders members of a rival drug ring.

And the judge has enunciated another principle that will guide his judgment:

> Everyone to whom much was given, of him much will be required, and from him to whom they entrusted much, they will demand the more. (Luke 12:48b)

A man with excellent brains and excellent physical health who uses his talents selfishly simply to accumulate wealth regardless of the sufferings of the poor, and makes no attempt to love his neighbour as himself, will be dealt with more severely than the poor, untalented man whose poverty made it impossible for him to help his neighbour (Luke 16:19–31).

The common destiny of the unrepentant and unbelieving

The *punishment* meted out, then, will vary from individual to individual. On the other hand, the *destiny* of all unrepentant and unbelieving people will be the same. It is described in Revelation 20:11–15 as both 'the second death' and as 'the lake of fire.'

(a) *The Second Death:* The second death is so called in order to distinguish it from physical death as we know it here on earth. Physical death is the door through which a human being passes into the (to us) unseen world, called in our passage Hades (which is Greek for 'unseen'). In that unseen world the spirits of the unrepenting and unbelieving are kept in custody, so to speak, awaiting the final judgment, in the same way as here on earth a criminal, when arrested, is kept on remand until he is brought up to court to stand trial before a judge (cf. Jude 6).

To prepare these spirits to stand trial, the final judgment will be preceded by the resurrection, and the spirits will be released from their temporary confinement and reunited with their resurrected bodies. This is what Revelation 20:13 refers to: 'And the sea gave up the dead who were in it,

Death and Hades gave up the dead who were in them.' The bodies of those drowned at sea (or whose ashes have been scattered upon the waves) will be resurrected; their spirits, released from their temporary confinement, will be reunited with their bodies. This is, of course, but one example of all who have died in various ways and places.

What happens then to those who are condemned at the final judgment? Will they be sentenced to go through the experience of physical death again? No. Physical death, the door by which they passed from our present world into the unseen world, will no longer have any function to perform. It shall give way to, and be superseded by, another and different kind of death, called in our passage the second death. And what kind of death will that be?

1. For the individual it will be a state of moral and spiritual death. Look again at what we learned in our previous chapter. The New Testament declares that each unregenerate person is already dead in this life, darkened in the understanding, and alienated from the life of God because of the hardening of the heart. Each is spiritually dead, intellectually beclouded, emotionally deadened (Eph 2:1-3; 4:17-19). Life on this earth gives opportunity to repent, to be reconciled to God, to be spiritually re-born, and to share the life of God both here and hereafter. But if a person throws away that opportunity, and passes through physical death into the eternal world, and is condemned at the final judgment, then the second death will fix him or her forever in that state of alienation from the life of God. It will not be annihilation; but a fixed and eternal spiritually morbid state, unrelieved by the life-giving mercy of God or by any hope of relief.

2. But it will be spiritual death not only for the individual, but for the whole society among whom he or she exists. Sin is not simply a spiritual disease from which an individual can suffer in total isolation from all other sinners. It also expresses itself in an individual's attitudes and behaviour towards others. People who in this life have been jealous, or envious, or lustful, or deceitful, or cruel, or proud, or aggressive, will not suddenly change into saints by going through physical death and appearing before the final judgment. Death works no magic. The Bible's description of the world-to-come is no fairy-tale. Imagine then what it will mean to live in such a society festering with such spiritual and moral disease, unmollified by the grace of God which once they could have received but which they have now finally and forever rejected.

The New Testament points out the blessedness of life with God and the redeemed in heaven by (among other things) contrasting it with the kind of society that will exist outside:

> Blessed are those who wash their robes, so that they may have the right to the tree of life and that they may enter the [heavenly] city by the gates. Outside are the dogs and sorcerers and the sexually immoral and murderers and idolaters, and everyone who loves and practises falsehood. (Rev 22:14–15)

(*b*) *The Lake of Fire:* The destiny of the unrepentant and unbelieving is also described as the Lake of Fire. Even if we assume that these terms are metaphorical and not literal, we may be sure they point to a reality that is far more terrible than any literal interpretation of the terms would convey.

There will be, in the first place, the pain of the conscious awareness of being under the displeasure of God (Rom 2:4-6). And in the second place, the pain of having to endure the consequences and outworkings of sinful attitudes and behaviour (Gal 6:7-8). And in the third place, there will be the anguish of remorse, compounded by unwillingness and inability to repent of the sin that gives rise to the remorse (Heb 6:4-8).

This fire will not annihilate the people that are in it, as literal earthly fire would. Our Lord Jesus described it in these terms: 'hell, where their worm dies not and the fire is not quenched' (Mark 9:47-48). When there is nothing left to burn, a fire goes out; and when a worm has nothing to feed on, it dies. But since the sinful attitudes of the lost will never change, the pain of God's displeasure which they attract shall never die away. And the memories that fuel the fires of remorse shall never be extinguished.

On the other hand, just as salt arrests corruption in meat, so, it seems, the eternal fire will stop the moral and spiritual corruption of the lost from increasing (Mark 9:48-49). As C. S. Lewis put it,

> God in His mercy made
> The fixèd pains of Hell.
> That misery might be stayed,
> God in His mercy made
> Eternal bounds and bade
> Its waves no further swell.[1]

1 *The Pilgrim's Regress* ([1933] London: Collins/Fount, 1977), 227.

The moral and spiritual corruption of each individual shall not be allowed to go on increasing indefinitely until it reaches infinite proportions. In God's mercy, it shall remain what it was at the final judgment. The 'fire' will restrain all further development.

CHAPTER 15

The Final Judgment

The Goodness and Severity of God

The thought that justice will eventually be done and wrongdoers punished ought to fill every right-minded person with profound satisfaction, if not jubilation. An ancient biblical poet put it this way:

> Sing praises to the Lord with the lyre . . . Let the rivers clap their hands; let the hills sing for joy together before the Lord, for he comes to judge the earth. He will judge the world with righteousness, and the peoples with equity. (Ps 98:5–9)

Even atheists who do not believe that there will be a final judgment ought to wish that there were one. They can surely not be glad that millions who have suffered injustice in life and died unjustly will, on their theory, never get justice at all.

And yet there is another side to the matter. While everybody is on the side of justice and our moral judgment agrees that justice must be done, the human heart has its own reasons and recoils at the very idea that any human being should be subjected to eternal punishment. The penalty seems unimaginably severe and disproportionate. Even human instinct would suggest that mercy ought to triumph over strict justice; and if we feel like that, ought not God by definition to feel that way even more so?

And then there is another reason why we recoil against the idea of a final judgment. It is simply this. Each one of us realizes that he too has sinned, and his sins, too, and not only the sins of notorious sinners, deserve to be punished. And when people realize this, they tend to start thinking up objections to try to prove to themselves that there could not be, and will not be, any such thing as eternal punishment. Let us examine some of these objections.

Objection 1

'A God of love would never punish anyone.'

First Answer: The very opposite is true. It is precisely because God is a God of love that he will punish sin. If a drug dealer jabs your daughter, gets her hooked on drugs and ruins her brain, God will never act as if it did not matter. He loves your daughter. Any sin against her incurs his wrath. And if the drug dealer never repents, God will never forget his crime, precisely because God's love is eternal. And that means that he will be wrathful against the drug dealer eternally.

Second Answer: God is indeed a God of love, and no one has ever told us more about the love of God and made us feel its reality more deeply than Jesus Christ. Perhaps the greatest and most famous expression of the love of God is:

> For God so loved the world, that he gave his only Son, that whoever believes in him should not perish but have eternal life. (John 3:16)

Yet in this verse we should notice that the love of God is exhibited supremely in what he has done to save us from perishing. He has given the greatest possible of all imaginable gifts, his own very substance, the Son of God himself. And he has given this gift so that sinful people like ourselves can be forgiven, and never have to suffer the punishment of their sins. But again the very fact that God had to go to such extreme lengths to save us from perishing must underline in our thinking the seriousness of what it would mean for anyone to perish.

The same impression is created by Christ's words:

> Truly, truly, I say to you, whoever hears my word and believes him who sent me has eternal life. He does not come into judgment, but has passed from death to life. (John 5:24)

Here he appeals for our faith and trust so that he may acquit us from all condemnation and save us from eternal death. We naturally ask what right he had to say this, and on what grounds he made his appeal. The answer is first that he made it as the one who is to be the judge at the final judgment:

> The Father judges no one, but has given all judgment
> to the Son . . . And he has given him authority to exe-
> cute judgment, because he is the Son of Man. (John
> 5:22, 27)

And in the second place, the answer is that the one who shall be judge at the final judgment is the very one who on the cross bore the penalty and punishment of God's law on behalf of all who will repent and believe, so that they might never have to bear the penalty and punishment themselves. But the unavoidable corollary of this is: if any disregard Christ's appeal for repentance and faith, they will inevitably perish.

At this point, therefore, we ought to look again at the passage that we studied in the last chapter and notice exactly what it says is the crucial factor that decides whether or not a person is cast into the lake of fire. Here are the relevant verses:

> Then I saw a great white throne and him who was
> seated on it. From his presence earth and sky fled away,
> and no place was found for them. And I saw the dead,
> great and small, standing before the throne, and books
> were opened. Then another book was opened, which
> is the book of life. And the dead were judged by what
> was written in the books, according to what they had
> done. . . . And if anyone's name was not found written
> in the book of life, he was thrown into the lake of fire.
> (Rev 20:11–15)

Notice first what it does not say. It does not say that if a person is found to have committed many, very bad sins, he is cast into the lake of fire; nor that if a person is found to have committed only a few smaller sins and has compensated for them by doing a lot of good works, he is not cast into the lake of fire. No, according to our passage the decisive factor is this: 'If anyone's name was not found written in the book of life, he was thrown into the lake of fire' (Rev 20:15).

This *book of life* is *the Lamb's book of life* (see Rev 21:27), and in that book are written the names of all those who have repented and put their faith in the Lamb of God. And since he paid the penalty of their sins for them, the New Testament gives them these glorious assurances: 'There is therefore now no condemnation for those who are in Christ Jesus. . . . much more shall [they] be saved by him from the wrath of God' (Rom 8:1; 5:8–9). And what is more, all those who have thus accepted Christ as their substitute and Saviour can know here and now in this life that their names are written in this book of life. The Apostle Paul and his friends did (Phil 4:3); and so may we.

If, however, people reject the Saviour whom God has provided, as alas many do, their names are not written in the Lamb's book of life. What then can God do to save them? They have made their own choice. Inevitably they will be cast into the lake of fire, and suffer the penalty and consequences of their sins. But they will have no one to blame but themselves. They certainly will not be able to criticize God for it. God is the sum total of all good. By definition there can be no alternative paradise for those who reject him. Nor is God under any moral obligation to provide the impossible. They loved darkness rather than light because their deeds were evil (John 3:19); and they will be given what they themselves have chosen.

Now let us notice another feature of God's justice. All who reject God's salvation will be alike in this, they will be cast into the lake of fire. But not all will endure the same severity of punishment. Our passage tells us that they will be judged according to their works. Even in a human court of justice, two men can be convicted and condemned to prison for a similar crime and yet receive different sentences because of mitigating circumstances in the one case and lack of them in the other. The genteel lady whose pride does not allow her to humble herself, repent and trust the Saviour, will suffer eternal loss, but she will not be punished with the same amount of suffering as, say, Hitler with the blood of millions on his hands.

Moreover, to see that God is fair and equal in all his dealings, let us recall another feature of his judgment. All who put their faith in Christ for salvation shall be saved eternally on the ground not of their works but of their faith. On the other hand, those who since their conversion have lived their lives to please God shall be rewarded for their good works, whereas those genuine believers who have nonetheless lived carelessly and produced works of substandard quality will suffer loss. Their unworthy works will be burned up, even though they themselves shall be saved, 'but only as by fire' (1 Cor 3:14–15).

Objection 2

'But millions of people in the centuries before Christ, and millions since, have never heard of Jesus. How would it be just of God to condemn them for not believing in Jesus?'

But he won't. God will never condemn anyone for not believing what he never heard (John 15:22-24). But all men know in their heart of hearts that there is a God. The universe offers ample evidence for his existence. And all men know in their consciences that they have sinned against God (Rom 1:18-2:16). Those who confess their sins and cast themselves on the mercy of God will be forgiven. The death and sacrifice of Jesus on the cross makes it perfectly just of God to forgive their sins even if they have never heard of Jesus (Rom 3:25). Men will therefore be judged by their response to what light they had, and not according to light which they never had.

But all who read this book have heard of Jesus, and they need to let him warn them that at the final judgment scrupulous care will be taken to assess what light each one had, and what opportunity to know the truth and to believe. According to Christ, those who have the most light are not those who necessarily make the right response. Many of the cultured and religious people among Christ's own contemporaries were less willing than pagan Gentiles to repent and believe (Luke 11:29-32).

Objection 3

'It would be unjust of God to punish someone for all eternity for sins, however large, that were committed during the brief period of a life of seventy or so years.'

But this objection is based on a double misapprehension:

1. It assumes that having sinned in this life, those who reject God and Christ will somehow cease to sin and be sinful in the world to come. That is not true.

2. It assumes that having refused to repent in this life, they would repent and trust the Saviour in the world to come. But that is not true, either. Those who have rejected the Saviour and defied God here, will go on rejecting the Saviour and defying God hereafter. They are guilty of an eternal sin (Mark 3:29). The rich man in the story which our Lord told (Luke 16:19–31) who found himself after death separated from God, and in torment showed evidence of remorse and anguish, but none of any genuine repentance.

Objection 4

'If all this were true, a God of love would compel people to repent and believe even against their will.'

No, he wouldn't. One of the things that distinguish human beings from animals and vegetables is the possession of free will. Man is a moral and spiritual being, made in the image of God, with the awesome power of choice either to love and obey his Creator or to reject him. God will not remove that free will from a human being, not even for the purpose of saving him. For if he did, what was saved would no longer be a human being, but an animal, vegetable, or even machine. Besides, God is no dictator. It is possible for a human being to reject and resist him, and to exist eternally.

Objection 5

'Concentrating people's minds on what is going to happen to them after death distracts and discourages them from making the most of their lives here on earth.'

The very opposite is true. Belief in heaven and hell invests every thought, attitude, and action in our lives on earth with infinite significance. It is refusal to believe in heaven and hell that revitalises and degrades man's moral and spiritual values.

Objection 6

'Only an unfeeling, inhuman monster would believe in and preach an eternal hell.'

But it was Jesus Christ who, more than any, taught us that God is love, that through his tears warned us of the reality of hell. He spoke more on this subject than anyone else in the whole of the Bible. He who died to save us from hell, warns us still that he did not die unnecessarily; and he laments over the unrepentant today as he once lamented over Jerusalem:

> O Jerusalem, Jerusalem, the city that kills the prophets and stones those who are sent to it! How often would I have gathered your children together as a hen gathers her brood under her wings, and you were not willing! (Luke 13:34 own trans.)

Through this lament of Christ's are heard the heartbeats of God our Creator: '"For I have no pleasure in the death of anyone," declares the Lord GOD; "so turn, and live"' (Ezek 18:32).

Our wisdom would therefore be to follow the example of those uncountable millions all down the centuries who have 'turned to God from idols to serve the living and true God, and to wait for his Son from heaven, whom he raised from the dead, Jesus who delivers us from the wrath to come' (1 Thess 1:9–10).

CHAPTER

Salvation

The Great Comprehensive Term

The concept of salvation is central to the New Testament; and the reason for that is obvious. When Christ was about to be born, Joseph, Mary's husband-to-be, was directed to call his name 'Jesus', the Greek form of a Hebrew name which means 'Yahweh saves'. This name was given to him, so the angel said, 'for he will save his people from their sins' (Matt 1:20–21). Salvation, then, was the very purpose of Christ's coming into the world: 'The Son of Man came to seek and to save the lost' (Luke 19:10; see also John 3:17; 1 Tim 1:15).

Understandably then, the words *salvation, Saviour, save* occur very frequently in the New Testament. Moreover, 'salvation' is a very broad, comprehensive term. It embraces many of the other terms, such as justification, ransom, regeneration, eternal life, etc., which we have already studied; for each of them defines one aspect of salvation.

Furthermore, the concept of salvation is often present in contexts where the word itself is not explicitly used. In the light of this, a study of 'salvation' will help us to review the ground we have covered in this book.

Its broad connotations

The Greek verb 'to save' (*sōzō*) carries several connotations. It can be used of rescuing someone from danger; or of delivering someone from illness, i.e. 'to heal'. In the Gospels we find Jesus saving people in these different senses. In response to Peter's appeal, 'Lord, save me', Christ rescues him from drowning (Matt 14:30–31). He heals a woman of a long-standing disease, and comments, 'Daughter, your faith has saved you; go in peace' (Luke 8:48 own trans.). He assured a man whose only daughter had just died, 'Only believe, and she shall be saved' and then proceeded to the man's house and raised his daughter from the dead (Luke 8:49–56).

Elsewhere, however, Christ uses the term 'save' in a moral and spiritual sense. For example, he said to a sinful, but repentant, woman: 'Your sins are forgiven. . . . Your faith has saved you; go in peace' (Luke 7:48, 50). Now it is in this sense that the words 'saved' and 'salvation' are most frequently used in the New Testament; and many of Christ's acts of physical healing and deliverance also serve as illustrations of salvation at the spiritual level.

In John 9, when our Lord gave sight to a man who had been born blind, Christ used this physical salvation as an illustration of his ability to give spiritual sight to the spiritually blind: 'And Jesus said, "For judgment I came into this world, that those who do not see may see, and those who see may become blind"' (John 9:39). It is in salvation at the moral and spiritual level that we shall be predominantly (though not exclusively) interested throughout the rest of this chapter.

Now because it is a comprehensive term denoting what God has done, is doing, and shall do for the believer, it is spoken of in three tenses: past, present, and future.

Salvation in the past tense

According to the New Testament, God desires all men to be saved, and to that end Christ has given himself a ransom for all men (1 Tim 2:3-6). The good news is, therefore, that salvation is available to all, though it becomes effective only when people believe. As soon as a person believes, however, he may rightly talk of his salvation as having now taken place. He need not confine himself to saying, 'I hope to be saved eventually.' He can rightly use the past tense and say, 'I have been saved.' Talking to believers, the New Testament says: 'By grace you have been saved' (Eph 2:5). That does not mean that believers have already experienced the *whole* of salvation, for some phases of salvation still lie in the future. But it remains true that certain phases of salvation are put into effect and completed the moment a person truly and personally commits himself to Christ.

Among these phases are:

1. Forgiveness: In the case of the sinful woman mentioned above, Christ used the perfect tense three times: 'Her sins, which are many, are forgiven ... Your sins are forgiven. ... Your faith has saved you' (Luke 7:47, 48, 50).

Similarly the Apostle John says: 'I am writing to you, little children, because your sins are forgiven for his name's sake' (1 John 2:12); and the Apostle Paul writes: God has 'forgiven all our trespasses' (Col 2:13).

Several metaphors are used in Scripture to impress on us the completeness of this forgiveness. God has put our sins:

(*a*) out of his sight: 'You have cast all my sins behind your back' (Isa 38:17);

(*b*) out of reach: 'As far as the east is from the west, so far does he remove our transgressions from us' (Ps 103:12);

(*c*) out of existence: 'I, I am he who blots out your transgressions' (Isa 43:25);

(*d*) beyond recall: 'I will remember their sin no more' (Jer 31:34);

(*e*) beyond recovery: 'Who is a God like you, pardoning iniquity . . . ; [you] will tread our iniquities underfoot. You will cast all our sins into the depths of the sea' (Mic 7:18–19).

2. Regeneration and New Spiritual Life (see Ch. 7):

(*a*) 'not because of works done by us in righteousness, but according to his own mercy, by the washing of regeneration and renewal of the Holy Spirit' (Titus 3:5).

(*b*) 'But God . . . even when we were dead in our trespasses, made us alive together with Christ . . . For by grace you have been saved through faith. And this is not your own doing; it is the gift of God, not a result of works, so that no one may boast' (Eph 2:4–9).

3. Reconciliation with God (see Ch. 4): 'More than that, we also rejoice in God through our Lord Jesus Christ, through whom we have now received reconciliation' (Rom 5:11).

Salvation in the present tense

Salvation not only concerns a person's past. It affects his present as well. A good example to start with is that of Zacchaeus (read his story in Luke 19:1–10). When salvation came to Zacchaeus's house, not only did it bring him forgiveness for the past, it drastically altered his lifestyle in the present. It began to activate his social conscience. Where he had extorted from people more tax than he was legally entitled to, he now offered to pay them back four times over. More than that. He could no longer be content to make a lot of money simply for himself, even legally, while many of his fellow citizens were poverty-stricken: 'The half of my goods', he said, 'I give to the poor.'

Concern for the poor, the ill, and the handicapped has always been the hallmark of true Christianity. Those, indeed, who have been saved through the gospel of Christ, are under bounden duty to behave in such a way in all life's relationships that they 'in everything they may adorn the doctrine of God our Saviour'; that is, they must demonstrate how attractive the gospel is by showing its practical effects on the way they live (Titus 2:10–14).

Here is another area in which salvation must control what a Christian does with his life. Christ put it this way: 'For whoever would save his life will lose it, but whoever loses his life for my sake and the gospel's will save it' (Mark 8:35). It will help us to begin to understand this statement, if we observe that the Greek word here translated 'soul' carries a wide range of meaning. It can mean one's physical life (as in Matt 2:20): 'Those who sought the child's life are dead.' It can also denote one's inner life, all that makes life more than just existence, one's love, energy, intellect, emotions, abilities, desires, ambitions (as in 3 John 2): 'I pray that . . . you may be in good [physical] health, as it goes well with your soul.' In Christ's statement (Mark 8:35) it carries both connotations, as we shall presently see.

But how can one save one's life, or soul, by losing it? It seems a contradiction. In fact it is possible to understand it only if we remember that this present age is not the only one there is: there is another, namely the coming kingdom of God. This was the context in which Christ taught the lesson: 'For whoever is ashamed of me and of my words in this adulterous and sinful generation, of him will the Son of Man also be ashamed when he comes in the glory of his Father with the holy angels' (Mark 8:38).

Christ had just predicted that the authorities at Jerusalem would put him to death. Peter, anticipating that if this happened, they might execute him as well, tried to persuade Christ to avoid execution. But Christ would not compromise his mission for the sake of saving his life. He warned Peter not to try to save his life in this world by denying Christ; if he did, he would lose it in the next. Peter, we know, did eventually lose his nerve and deny Christ. But this was only a temporary lapse from which Christ restored him by his intercessions (Luke 22:31–34).

But the lesson remains for us all. Admittedly, we do not earn salvation by being martyred for Christ. Salvation is a free gift. But we cannot have the gift of salvation without the Saviour. 'For', says Scripture, 'it has been granted to you that for the sake of Christ you should not only believe in him but also suffer for his sake' (Phil 1:29). Suppose, then, we ever face the situation where we have to choose: either we deny and renounce Christ and save our physical life in this world, or we maintain our faith in Christ, remain loyal to him, and lose our life in this world. Then we must be prepared to lose our life in this world, assured that we shall save it in the world to come; whereas, if we save our life in this world by denying Christ, we shall lose it in the world to come.

Moreover life in this world is not a thing which we can put in a box for safekeeping. A life has to be lived: its energies, time, ambitions, love, abilities have to be spent on people or things or projects. The question is: on what shall we spend them?

A believer is called on to do all he does heartily as to the Lord (Col 3:23) and to devote as much of his time and energy as he can to the furtherance of Christ's gospel. If he sets out to spend his life this way, sooner or later it will involve him in all kinds of sacrifice and self-denial. To a worldly-minded man, the believer will appear to be wasting his life and throwing it away. But in actual fact everything that a believer does for Christ or spends on Christ and on his interests, attains permanent and eternal significance. Its results will last forever (John 12:25).

If, on the other hand, the believer is not prepared to live for Christ, and spends his time, energy, love, abilities selfishly on himself and on merely worldly and unworthy things, then as far as God's eternal kingdom is concerned, all that the believer has spent on these worldly things is lost forever. And when Christ at his second coming examines this man's works, his works will be burned up and he shall suffer loss, even though he himself shall be saved (1 Cor 3:10–15).

Salvation in the future tense

While a believer may with confidence say, 'I have been saved', important parts of his salvation still lie in the future. That is why the believer is said to hope for them. Not because they are uncertain but simply because they are not yet present.

He may rightly speak about them with equal confidence and humbly assert, 'I shall be saved'. These future aspects of salvation include:

1. *Salvation from the wrath of God:* 'Since, therefore, we have now been justified by his blood, much more shall we be saved by him from the wrath of God' (Rom 5:9; see also 1 Thess 5:9-10).

2. *The redemption of our physical bodies:* This also is something that will take place at the second coming of Christ.

(*a*) 'But our citizenship is in heaven, and from it we await a Saviour, the Lord Jesus Christ, who will transform our lowly body to be like his glorious body, by the power that enables him even to subject all things to himself' (Phil 3:20-21).

(*b*) 'And not only the creation, but we ourselves, who have the firstfruits of the Spirit, groan inwardly as we wait eagerly for adoption as sons, the redemption of our bodies. For in this hope we were saved. Now hope that is seen is not hope. For who hopes for what he sees? But if we hope for what we do not see, we wait for it with patience' (Rom 8:23-25).

3. *The Christian's final sanctification* (see Ch. 14):

(*a*) 'Blessed be the God and Father of our Lord Jesus Christ! According to his great mercy, he has caused us to be born again to a living hope through the resurrection of Jesus Christ from the dead, to an inheritance that is imperishable, undefiled, and unfading, kept in heaven for you' (see 1 Pet 1:3-4).

(b) 'When Christ who is your life appears, then you also will appear with him in glory' (Col 3:4).

4. *The Christian's entry into heaven:* A believer's entry into heaven can occur in one of two ways. Those who die before the Lord comes again are said to be 'away from the body and at home with the Lord' (2 Cor 5:8) even though their physical body has not yet been raised. Then at the Lord's coming the dead bodies of these believers will be raised, the bodies of the believers who are still alive will be changed, and all will be caught up to meet the Lord in the air (1 Thess 4:13-18).

> Behold! I tell you a mystery. We shall not all sleep, but we shall all be changed, in a moment, in the twinkling of an eye, at the last trumpet. For the trumpet will sound, and the dead will be raised imperishable, and we shall be changed. . . . When the perishable puts on the imperishable, and the mortal puts on immortality, then shall come to pass the saying that is written: 'Death is swallowed up in victory.' (1 Cor 15:51-52, 54)

It is in this sense that Scripture says: 'salvation is nearer to us now than when we first believed' (Rom 13:11)— nearer, because with every passing day the second coming of Christ grows nearer still.

We have now reached the end of our brief survey of some key biblical concepts. We trust that these explanations have enabled you to understand clearly what the central message of the Bible is. We also dare to hope that the reasons we have given for why we believe the Christian message to be wonderfully true will encourage you to continue to explore that message and enter into the new life that is promised to all those who place their trust in Jesus Christ as Saviour and Lord. In the end it will be the taking of that step of faith that gives rise to the final personal confirmation that Christianity is true.

Scripture Index

OLD TESTAMENT

Genesis
1   *76*
1:31   *17*
3   *26, 32–3*
3:1–7   *106–7*

Exodus
34:5–7   *17*

Leviticus
19:2   *16*
19:18   *16–17*

Deuteronomy
6:13   *13*
25:1   *39*

1 Samuel
2:2   *12*

1 Chronicles
16:29   *12*

Psalms
43:4   *11*
92:15   *14*
98:5–9   *138*
103:12   *151*

Proverbs
17:15   *40*
30:20   *49*

Isaiah
5:7–30   *15*
5:15–16   *15*
5:16   *15*
5:24   *15*
6:3   *15*
6:5   *15–16*
38:17   *151*
43:3   *19*
43:11   *79*
43:25   *151*
45:11–12   *13*
45:18   *13*
45:20–22   *19*
46:1–7   *12*

53:4–6   *99–100*
53:5   *19*
53:6   *68*
53:10–12   *99–100*
54:5   *19*
55:7–8   *67*

Jeremiah
31:34   *151*

Ezekiel
11:19–20   *108*
18:32   *146*

Micah
7:18–19   *151*

NEW TESTAMENT

Matthew
1:20–21   *148*
2:20   *152*
3:8   *73*
3:10   *70*
4:10   *13*

Scripture Index

Matthew

5:23–24 *32*
5:33–37 *84*
5:43–48 *121*
14:30–31 *149*
15 *113*
27:3–5 *66*
27:11–26 *23*
27:62–66 *95*
28:1–10 *97*
28:11–15 *95*
28:16–20 *97*

Mark

1:15 *65*
3:29 *145*
8:35 *153*
8:38 *153*
9:47–48 *136*
9:48–49 *136*
10:45 *52*

Luke

6:43–44 *70*
7:29 *39*
7:47 *150*
7:48 *149, 150*
7:50 *149, 150*
8:48 *149*
8:49–56 *149*
9:22 *56*
11:29–32 *144*
12:4 *56*
12:47–48 *132*
12:48 *132*
13:3 *73*

13:5 *73*
13:34 *146*
15 *38*
15:10 *65*
15:32 *59–60*
16:19–31 *133, 145*
16:25 *131*
18:9–14 *41*
19:1–10 *152*
19:10 *148*
22:31–34 *153*
22:31–32 *109*
23:1–25 *23*
24 *97*

John

1:1–4 *76*
1:1–3 *13*
2:13–16 *49*
3:16 *62, 140*
3:17 *27–8*
3:17 *148*
3:19 *142–3*
3:36 *58*
5:22 *132, 141*
5:24 *45, 140*
5:27–29 *132*
5:27 *141*
5:36 *82*
6 *85*
6:26 *85*
6:28–58 *86*
6:35 *87*
7:1–7 *88*
7:16–17 *78*
8:13 *80*

8:14 *80*
8:28 *90*
8:31–36 *86*
9 *149*
9:39 *149–50*
10:11 *91*
10:14–17 *91*
10:28 *62*
12:25 *64, 154*
13:6–11 *115*
14:6 *84*
15:22–24 *144*
15:24 *82*
16:1–3 *56*
16:7–14 *99*
16:28 *99*
18:28–19:16 *23*
17:1–3 *56*
17:3 *61*
17:17 *126*
19:8–12 *24*
20:1–10 *94*
20:11–18 *97*
20:19–23 *97*
20:30–31 *78, 83*
21 *97*

Acts

1:4–9 *99*
1:21–22 *99*
2:36–39 *32*
2:38 *99*
4:12 *102*
9 *96*
9:32 *111*
11:18 *65–6*

Acts
15:8-9   *114*
17:30   *73*
20:21   *67, 73, 74*
20:28   *55*

Romans
1:14-16   *51*
1:18-2:16   *144*
1:27   *14-15*
2:4-6   *136*
2:14-15   *129*
2:16   *131*
3:10-18   *22-23*
3:19-28   *119-20*
3:19   *42-3*
3:20   *43*
3:23-26   *44*
3:23   *42, 69*
3:25   *144*
3:28   *45, 103*
4:5   *103*
5:1-2   *127*
5:1   *45*
5:5   *114*
5:6-11   *28*
5:6   *23*
5:8-9   *142*
5:9   *155*
5:11   *35, 151*
5:19   *28*
6:1-2   *120*
6:3-4   *70*
6:6-11   *124*
6:8-11   *71*
6:14   *124*

6:15   *120*
6:16-23   *54*
6:23   *62*
7:4   *124*
7:5   *25-6*
7:6   *125*
7:7-25   *120-1*
7:7-9   *25-6*
7:7-8   *122*
7:12   *121*
7:15   *122*
7:18-19   *122*
7:19   *21*
7:21-24   *122*
7:22   *122*
7:23   *122*
7:25   *122*
8:1   *142*
8:3   *122*
8:4   *124*
8:7   *25*
8:13-17   *121*
8:14-17   *114, 126*
8:18-25   *55*
8:23-25   *155*
8:26-30   *126*
10:9   *74*
12:1-2   *116*
13:11   *156*

1 Corinthians
1:2   *111*
1:18   *87*
1:22-23   *87*
1:30   *118*
2:2   *87*

2:5   *87*
3:10-15   *154*
3:14-15   *143*
6:11   *111*
6:15-17   *71*
6:16-17   *124-5*
6:19-20   *117*
9:24-27   *64*
10:13   *108-9*
15:3-8   *97*
15:3-4   *100*
15:20-23   *93*
15:51-52   *156*
15:54   *156*

2 Corinthians
4:17   *62*
5:1   *62*
5:8   *57, 156*
5:14-15   *116-17*
5:18-21   *31*
5:19-21   *34*
6:1   *37*
7:1   *119*
7:10   *66*

Galatians
2:19-21   *71*
2:20   *72*
3:10-12   *102*
3:13   *50*
5:16-24   *126*
5:19-21   *22*
6:7-8   *136*
6:8   *63, 126*

Ephesians
1:7 *50*
1:13–14 *55*
2:1–3 *69, 134*
2:4–9 *151*
2:4–5 *60*
2:5 *150*
2:8–10 *108*
2:8–9 *103*
2:11–18 *36*
2:18 *115*
3:5 *110–11*
4:17–24 *120*
4:17–19 *134*

Philippians
1:23 *57*
1:29 *153*
3:12 *127*
3:20–21 *55, 155*
4:3 *142*

Colossians
1:14–17 *52*
1:15–22 *31*
1:17 *12*
1:20 *37*
1:21 *25*
2:13–15 *51*
2:13 *151*
3:4 *156*
3:23 *154*

1 Thessalonians
1:9–10 *146–7*
1:9 *68*

4:13–18 *156*
5:9–10 *155*

1 Timothy
1:9–11 *24*
1:12–17 *25*
1:15 *27, 148*
2:3–6 *90–1, 150*
2:5–6 *52, 101–2*
4:7–8 *63*
6:11–12 *63*
6:12–16 *109*

2 Timothy
2:5 *64*
2:13 *54*
4:7–8 *109*

Titus
1:2 *54*
2:10–14 *152*
2:11–14 *54–5*
3:5 *114, 151*

Hebrews
5:9 *62*
6:1 *67*
6:4–8 *136*
7:25 *109*
9:11–12 *50*
9:12 *62*
9:13–14 *112, 113*
9:15 *62*
9:27 *45, 130*
10:5 *112–13*
10:7 *112–13*

10:10 *112–13*
10:11–12 *102*
10:14 *115*
10:19–22 *115*
11 *108*
11:3 *76*
12:1–13 *126–7*
12:1 *63*

James
2:10 *42*
2:19 *80*
2:24 *45*

1 Peter
1:2 *114*
1:3–4 *92, 156*
1:6–7 *108*
1:8 *93*
1:14–16 *115*
1:18–19 *52*
1:18 *48*
1:21 *92*
2:5 *116*
2:9–10 *16, 116*
3:14–15 *13–14*

2 Peter
1:1–11 *125*
1:5–11 *64*
3:2 *110–11*
3:9 *90*

1 John
1:1–4 *61*
1:5 *14*

1 John
1:7   *113*
1:9   *73, 124*
2:12   *151*
2:21   *84*
3:2   *127*
3:4   *27*
3:16   *91*
4:10   *53*
4:16   *17*
4:18   *91*
4:19   *116*
5:1   *118*
5:9–13   *105–6*
5:10   *107*
5:11–13   *64*

5:11   *106*

3 John
2   *152–3*

Jude
6   *133*

Revelation
1:5–6   *115*
2:5   *73*
2:16   *73*
2:21   *73*
3:3   *73*
4:8–11   *13*
5:9–10   *115*

5:11–14   *37*
20:11–15   *58, 129–30, 133, 141*
20:12   *131*
20:13   *133*
20:15   *142*
21:27   *142*
22:14–15   *135*

OTHER ANCIENT LITERATURE
Lucretius
De Rerum Natura
Book 1   *89*

Other books by David Gooding
(published by Myrtlefield House)

Myrtlefield Expositions
The Riches of Divine Wisdom (NT use of OT)
According to Luke (The Third Gospel)
In the School of Christ (John 13–17)
True to the Faith (Acts of the Apostles)
An Unshakeable Kingdom (Letter to the Hebrews)

Myrtlefield Discoveries
How to Teach the Tabernacle
Windows on Paradise (Gospel of Luke)

Other books by John Lennox

Determined to Believe? (Monarch, 2018)
Can Science Explain Everything?
(The Good Book Company, 2019)
*Joseph: A Story of Love, Hate, Slavery,
Power, and Forgiveness* (Crossway, 2019)
*Against the Flow: The inspiration of Daniel
in an age of relativism* (Monarch, 2015)
God's Undertaker: Has Science Buried God? (Lion, 2009)
Gunning for God: A Critique of the New Atheism (Lion, 2011)
Miracles: Is Belief in the Supernatural Irrational?
VeriTalks Vol. 2. (The Veritas Forum, 2013)
Seven Days That Divide the World (Zondervan, 2011)

The Quest for Reality and Significance

*A Six Part Series
by David Gooding and John Lennox*

We need a coherent picture of our world. Life's realities won't let us ignore its fundamental questions, but with so many opposing views, how will we choose answers that are reliable? In this series of books, David Gooding and John Lennox offer a fair analysis of religious and philosophical attempts to find the truth about the world and our place in it. By listening to the Bible alongside other leading voices, they show that it is not only answering life's biggest questions—it is asking better questions than we ever thought to ask.

Different Ways of Expressing Truth

(An excerpt from *Questioning Our Knowledge*)

Different ways of expressing truth

It is plain to see that in the Bible there are, in the sense we earlier discussed, different kinds of truth or, better said, different ways of conveying truth.

Poetic truth or truth expressed through poetry

Not only are the books of Job and Psalms written as poetry, but so are major parts of the prophetic books like Isaiah and Jeremiah; and we interpret them accordingly. In the famous shepherd psalm, David says:

> You prepare a table before me in the presence of my enemies; you anoint my head with oil; my cup overflows. (Ps 23:5)

The language, taken literally, describes a banquet provided by a host who would anoint the head of each guest with perfumed ointment and see to it that his glass was constantly filled. But no one supposes that David is here talking of a literal banquet. Yet what he says is nonetheless a truthful expression of God's care and provision for him that he had experienced in the desert, when he was being persecuted by King Saul.

Similarly, when the psalmist describes the absolute completeness of God's forgiveness by remarking: 'As far as the east is from the west, so far does he remove our transgressions from us' (Ps 103:12), he is not implying that sin and guilt are entities that can be removed and placed at an enormous physical distance from us. He is expressing in vivid figurative language the truth that when God forgives, he promises never to rake up again the guilt of our sin and haunt us with it (see the same thing said in straightforward language in Heb 10:17).

Propositional truth

In this connection special interest attaches to the so-called 'amen-formula' with which Christ introduced many of his statements. *ʾāmēn* is a Hebrew word, connected with a verb that carries the idea of affirmation and certainty. So, for instance, if a priest or judge put a person on oath and repeated the terms of the oath and the solemn consequences that would follow perjury, the person concerned would respond with the word *ʾāmēn*. He or she thus affirmed the oath, and agreed to its terms. Similarly, at the end of a public prayer or confession the congregation would say 'amen', thus affirming their agreement. And since, when people took an oath before God, they were appealing to God to witness their oath, God is sometimes referred to in the Old Testament as 'God of the Amen' (cf. Isa 65:16); translated in many languages as 'God of Truth'.

Christ was unusual in that when he made solemn statements, whether propositions or promises, he frequently *prefaced* (not ended) those statement with the word *ămēn*, often repeating it in order to lay double emphasis on their utter truthfulness and certainty. Examples are:

> Amen, amen, I say to you, unless one is born again, he cannot see the kingdom of God. (John 3:3)

> Amen, amen, I say to you, whoever hears my word and believes him who sent me has eternal life. He does not come into judgment, but has passed from death to life. (John 5:24)

Now, as we have said, *ămēn* is a Hebrew word, and the New Testament was written in Greek. Naturally, therefore, in the New Testament Christ's words are normally translated into Greek. But the apostles were obviously so impressed with Christ's repeated emphatic affirmation of the truthfulness of his statements that, in recording them, they have often simply transliterated the Hebrew word *ămēn*, rather than translate it. That means that as we now read these words, we are reading the actual words spoken by Christ, as J. Jeremias demonstrated.[1]

---

[1] *New Testament Theology*, 35–6.

Similarly, at Revelation 3:14 Christ applies the term *āmēn* not only to his statements and promises but to himself: 'The words of the Amen, the faithful and true witness'. Faith, therefore, in the statements, propositions and promises uttered by Christ and God is regarded as being ultimately based on a person's estimate of the moral character and trustworthiness of Christ and God. One cannot separate the truthfulness of the statements from the truthfulness of the persons who make them. So, for instance, in a famous passage the Christian apostle, John, first argues that not to believe a statement made by God is to call into question God's personal truthfulness:

> Whoever does not believe God has made him a liar, because he has not believed in the testimony that God has borne concerning his Son. (1 John 5:10)

And then John cites the statements that God has made and expects people to believe simply on the ground that God has made them:

> And this is the testimony, that God gave us eternal life, and this life is in his Son. Whoever has the Son has the life; whoever does not have the Son of God does not have life. (1 John 5:11–12)

Truths expressed in precise legal language

At various places the Old Testament takes the forms of a legal covenant. When these covenants are interpreted in the New Testament great emphasis is laid on the precise wording of the original covenant and on exact representation of its terms. An example is:

> To give a human example, brothers: even with a man-made covenant, no one annuls it or adds to it once it has been ratified. Now the promises were made to Abraham and to his offspring [lit. 'seed']. It does not say 'And to his offsprings [lit. 'seeds']', referring to many, but referring to one, 'And to your offspring [seed]', who is Christ. This is what I mean: the law, which came 430 years afterwards, does not annul a covenant previously ratified by God, so as to make the promise void. (Gal 3:15–17)

Existential truth

The Bible records not only propositional statements of Christian doctrine, but also the testimony of people who claim to have proved these doctrines to be true in their own practical experience. A good example is that of Paul, the Christian apostle, who first relates his own experience and then on that basis, asserts his conviction of the truth and trustworthiness of Christian doctrine:

> formerly I was a blasphemer, persecutor, and inso-
> lent opponent. But I received mercy . . . and the
> grace of our Lord overflowed for me with faith
> and love that are in Christ Jesus. The saying is
> trustworthy and deserving of full acceptance, that
> Christ Jesus came into the world to save sinners, of
> whom I am foremost. (1 Tim 1:13–15)

Revealed truth

In a number of places the New Testament uses the term
'the truth' to denote the body of divinely revealed truth
in regard to:

Creation

> men, who . . . suppress the truth . . . For what can
> be known about God is plain to them, because God
> has shown it to them. For his invisible attributes,
> namely, his eternal power and divine nature, have
> been clearly perceived, ever since the creation of
> the world, in the things that have been made . . .
> they exchanged the truth about God for a lie and
> worshipped and served the creature rather than
> the Creator. (Rom 1:18–20, 25)

Here lies the basic difference between atheism and
theism. To the atheist the universe is not a revelation of
anything. It is simply a brute fact with nothing to tell us

about anything outside itself. One can study what it is made of, how it works, and one can deduce the regular principles its working seems to follow and call these principles laws. But one is not allowed to ask whether the universe reveals a creative Mind behind its existence because by definition, according to atheism, there is no Mind behind the universe for it to reveal.

The Bible, by contrast, asserts that the universe is the vehicle of God's self-revelation of his power and divine nature; and that to regard the universe itself as the Ultimate Reality, and the matter and forces of nature as the Ultimate Powers, is the Fundamental Falsehood in contradistinction to the Fundamental Truth about the universe and our place and significance in it.

The Bible further predicts that when atheism finally produces its fully developed harvest, its fundamental falsehood that there is no God will develop into the further falsehood that man, the highest product of evolution, is God and should act as God (2 Thess 2:3–4, 9–12). It will be the final logical outworking of the deception early instilled, according to the Bible, into mankind's heart and imagination: *'you shall be as God'* (Gen 3:5).

The gospel

> when you heard the word of truth, the gospel of your salvation (Eph 1:13)

> so that the truth of the gospel might be preserved for you (Gal 2:5)

> Who hindered you from obeying the truth? (Gal
> 5:7)

From these few examples, and many others like them, it is evident in the New Testament that 'the truth of the gospel' and 'the truth' (*tout court*) often refer to the same thing. Truth is essentially the revealed truth of the gospel message. So to believe the gospel and thus become a Christian is 'to come to the knowledge of the truth' (cf. 1 Tim 2:4; 2 Tim 3:7). As to the origin and the communication of this gospel, the New Testament talks in this fashion:

> When the Spirit of truth comes, he will guide you
> into all the truth. (John 16:13)

> the gospel that was preached by me is not man's
> gospel. For I did not receive it from any man, nor
> was I taught it, but I received it through a revela-
> tion of Jesus Christ. (Gal 1:11–12)

The gospel, as being truth, is also distinguished from myth and legend. Foreseeing what would happen all too often in the subsequent centuries Paul remarks:

> For the time is coming when people will not
> endure sound teaching, but ... will turn away
> from listening to the truth and wander off into
> myths. (2 Tim 4:3–4)

Christ is himself the truth

For a true understanding of the Christian gospel, it is important to notice that Christ not only claimed to *teach* the truth: he claimed to *be* the truth. He was the Son of God, in what the theologians call hypostatic union with the Father; and though he became truly human, he never ceased to be God. He was simultaneously God and man. He was, therefore, God revealing himself in human form:

> No one has ever seen God; the only God [or, 'the only One, who is God'], who is at the Father's side, he has made him known. (John 1:18)

> Whoever has seen me has seen the Father. (John 14:9)

> I am the way, and the truth, and the life. No one comes to the Father except through me. (John 14:6)

> He is the radiance of the glory of God and the exact imprint of his nature. (Heb 1:3)

> By him all things were created, in heaven and on earth, visible and invisible . . . all things were created through him and for him. (Col 1:16)

Since everything in heaven and earth was created by God and for God, the ultimate truth about everything—about its origin, maintenance and goal—is God. According to the Bible, Christ is that God incarnate (i.e. in the flesh). In Christ we have eternal truth and historical truth, eternal truth expressed in time and historical truth of eternal significance. The historical facts of the life, death and resurrection of Christ are the truth about God. To know the only true God and Jesus Christ, the Son of the Father, is to experience eternal life already begun here in time (John 17:3). So John, who at the Last Supper reclined at table next to Jesus, subsequently writes:

> And we know that the Son of God has come and has given us understanding, so that we may know him who is true; and we are in him who is true, in his Son Jesus Christ. He is the true God and eternal life. Little children, keep yourselves from idols. (1 John 5:20–21)

Now, of course, not everyone accepts that Jesus is the truth, nor did they when he first made his claims. The opposition to his claims was at times severe, culminating ultimately in his arrest, trial and crucifixion. The issues involved in that trial speak to the question of truth directly and are the subject of our next chapter.

Being Truly Human

*The Limits of Our Worth, Power,
Freedom and Destiny*

In Book 1 – *Being Truly Human*, Gooding and Lennox address issues surrounding the value of humans. They consider the nature and basis of morality, compare what morality means in different systems, and assess the dangerous way freedom is often devalued. What should guide our use of power? What should limit our choices? And to what extent can our choices keep us from fulfilling our potential?

Finding Ultimate Reality

*In Search of the Best Answers
to the Biggest Questions*

In Book 2 – *Finding Ultimate Reality*, Gooding and Lennox remind us that the authority behind ethics cannot be separated from the truth about ultimate reality. Is there a Creator who stands behind his moral law? Are we the product of amoral forces, left to create moral consensus? Gooding and Lennox compare ultimate reality as understood in: Indian Pantheistic Monism, Greek Philosophy and Mysticism, Naturalism and Atheism, and Christian Theism.

Questioning Our Knowledge

*Can We Know What
We Need to Know?*

In Book 3 – *Questioning Our Knowledge,* Gooding and Lennox discuss how we could know whether any of these competing worldviews are true. What is truth anyway, and is it absolute? How would we recognize truth if we encountered it? Beneath these questions lies another that affects science, philosophy, ethics, literature and our everyday lives: how do we know anything at all?

Doing What's Right

*Whose System of Ethics
is Good Enough?*

In Book 4 – *Doing What's Right*, Gooding and Lennox present particular ethical theories that claim to hold the basic principles everyone should follow. They compare the insights and potential weaknesses of each system by asking: what is its authority, its supreme goal, its specific rules, and its guidance for daily life? They then evaluate why even the best theories have proven to be impossible to follow consistently.

Claiming to Answer

*How One Person Became the Response
to Our Deepest Questions*

In Book 5 – *Claiming to Answer*, Gooding and Lennox
argue it is not enough to have an ethical theory telling us what standards we ought to live by, because
we often fail in our duties and do what we know is
wrong. How can we overcome this universal weakness? Many religions claim to be able to help, but is
the hope they offer true? Gooding and Lennox state
why they think the claims of Jesus Christ are valid
and the help he offers is real.

Suffering Life's Pain

Facing the Problems of Moral and Natural Evil

In Book 6 – *Suffering Life's Pain*, Gooding and Lennox acknowledge the problem with believing in a wise, loving and just God who does not stop natural disasters or human cruelty. Why does he permit congenital diseases, human trafficking and genocide? Is he unable to do anything? Or does he not care? Gooding and Lennox offer answers based on the Creator's purpose for the human race, and his entry into his own creation.

About the Authors

David W. Gooding is Professor Emeritus of Old Testament Greek at Queen's University Belfast and a Member of the Royal Irish Academy. He has taught the Bible internationally and lectured on both its authenticity and its relevance to philosophy, world religions and daily life. He has published scholarly articles on the Septuagint and Old Testament narratives, as well as expositions of Luke, John, Acts, Hebrews, the New Testament's Use of the Old Testament, and several books addressing arguments against the Bible and the Christian faith. His analysis of the Bible and our world continues to shape the thinking of scholars, teachers and students alike.

John C. Lennox, is Professor Emeritus of Mathematics at the University of Oxford and Emeritus Fellow in Mathematics and the Philosophy of Science at Green Templeton College. He is also an Associate Fellow of the Said Business School, University of Oxford. In addition, he is an Adjunct Lecturer at the Oxford Centre for Christian Apologetics, as well as being a Senior Fellow of the Trinity Forum. In addition to academic works, he has published on the relationship between science and Christianity, the books of Genesis and Daniel, and the doctrine of divine sovereignty and human free will. He has lectured internationally and participated in a number of televised debates with some of the world's leading atheist thinkers.